Iona L. Anderson

THE EFFECTIVENESS OF AN OPEN CLASSROOM APPROACH ON SECOND LANGUAGE ACQUISITION

San Francisco, California
1978

Published by

R & E RESEARCH ASSOCIATES, INC.
4843 Mission Street
San Francisco, California 94112

Publishers

Robert D. Reed and Adam S. Eterovich

Library of Congress Card Catalog Number

78-62238

I.S.B.N.

0-88247-541-X

ACKNOWLEDGMENTS

Acknowledgments are due several persons who persevered with me from the initial stage to the completion of my study. Firstly, I should like to thank my three supportive advisors for their faith in me, their patience, endurance, encouragement,and for recommending valuable sources of information for the study.

Secondly, I should like to thank Dr. Morsely Giddings for taking time to listen to my concerns, give immediate guidance, suggestions and advice.

Thirdly, I should like to thank the many New York City public school faculty and staff, parents and children who cooperated in bringing this study to a successful conclusion.

TABLE OF CONTENTS

LIST OF TABLES

LIST OF FIGURES

CHAPTER I

INTRODUCTION

Of the many innovations in the past decade showing successes in the demand for more effective, humanistic, and flexible models for change in education, teaching English to speakers of other languages, open education, and competency based teacher education programs are a few of the many educational priorities demanding a closer look. Plans for this research study primarily developed out of the author's years of interest in second language acquisition and secondarily just how learning a second language could best be achieved.

The theory behind second language learning is best described by Lado (1964) who defined second language as "acquiring the ability to use its structure within a general vocabulary under essentially the conditions of normal communication among native speakers at conversational speed" (p. 38). Learning the expressions of a second language, the content and the association of the two for rapid use in proper positions are the goals set by those teaching a second language. How to achieve these goals seemed more feasible with the emergence of new organizational patterns in the schools. One new emerging pattern called the "open classroom" was designed to consider the "total child" developing in a natural, social environment where communication, verbal and nonverbal, is always taking place.

Nyquist and Hawes (1972) defined the open classroom as:

The environment we seek to create within the schools is one which is truly responsive to the needs and the interest of children; in which children's learning is deeply rooted in experience, where the children in an atmosphere of mutual trust and respect can carry on with each other and with adults the kind of open dialogue that is the essence of good education. (p. 67)

Blitz (1973) also wrote on child development

the essential thought behind the open classroom is that children are unique, physically active individuals and that their learning needs can only be met in a free, active atmosphere which tailors the learning environment to specific needs and abilities of each child. (p. 4)

There is a high correlation between the goals of second language acquisition and the learning environment in which this can take place. It was this phenomenon that led to the research reported in this investigation. Indications and initial informed expectations suggested that second language learners would develop communicative competence in an open classroom beyond that level which it might have ordinarily been achieved in a traditional, i.e., non-innovative, elementary school classroom. Further indications were that the language learner rated "C" on the New York City Language Rating Scale (which is to be described in comprehensive terms in Chapter III of this dissertation)

1

would have the opportunity to practice language in all of its forms. This child has special language needs important to his progress in reading.

Statement of the Problem

The major purpose of this study was to compare second language acquisition in an open classroom environment with second language acquisition in a traditional environment. Specifically, the study sought to explore how a second language learner developed intellectually in a child centered setting as compared with language development in a traditional setting. This study explored the encoding and decoding processes in second language development as well as those unique aspects of the socialization process which were thought to be intimately involved in the development of such competence. In searching for answers to the problems of second language acquisition, the following questions were posed:

1. In what way does language instruction for the second language learner in the open classroom differ from the formal auraloral language instruction given in traditional classrooms?

2. What is the relationship between the organizational plan of the open classroom and the achievement of communicative competence and linguistic competence?

3. What are the differences in achievement between the two groups from the pretest and posttest scores of the New York City Language Rating Scale and a Cloze reading test?

4. How did second language learners in the fourth grade grow cognitively in the open classroom?

Key Concepts

For the sake of clarity several terms used in the development of the study need to be defined.

1. Aural-oral - a term used to describe an instructional method used in teaching second language through the language arts sequence of listening first and then speaking, hearing, and then saying. The second language learner is expected to imitate, repeat and practice what has been modeled by the teacher.

2. Cloze Reading Test - a method of systematically deleting words from a prose selection and then evaluating the comprehension level and readability level of a reader who must supply the words deleted. The results determine a student's frustration level, educable level, or competence level. This method has been considered reliable in testing the reading comprehension level of second language learners.

3. Communicative competence - a term used to describe the ability of the second language learner to effectively use language in situations where he must communicate in a social conversational way, thus understanding a speaker and being understood by a speaker. It is also defined as "the ability to produce or understand utterances which are appropriate to the context in which they are made" (Campbell & Wales, 1970, p. 247).

4. Decode - a term used by linguists to define the reading process in which the sounds which the printed symbols represent are put back into spoken form (Aukerman, 1971, p. 147).

5. Encode - a term used in linguistics meaning to transfer from one system of human communication into another. One must convert to a code that represents learning behaviors of a social community when

2

speaking or writing.

6. <u>English as a Second Language</u> (ESL) - is a term used to define the ability of a second language learner to use English structure and vocabulary in communicating in an English speaking environment.

7. <u>Language</u> - is a term used to describe a complex system of communication that people use out of habit to convey cultural experiences. Logan, Logan and Patterson (1972) defined language in these terms - "Language is a social phenomenon, as well as a social institution. It serves to integrate cultures, to bind people together in a common approach to living. Language as structure confronts the students as does language as process" (p. 243). A language "is both a component of culture and a central network through which the other components are expressed" (Lado, 1964, p. 23).

8. <u>Language learner</u> - a term applied to a student whose native language is not the language of instruction or the language of the majority population in the broader community - a student rated "C" or below on the New York City Language Rating Scale is classified as a language learner.

9. <u>Linguistics</u> - a term used to describe a study based on a scientific investigation of languages and the nature of language. The study observes speech, describes it, classifies it and presents its structure as completely and as accurately as possible.

10. <u>Linguistic competence</u> - a term used to describe the ability of a second language learner to effectively use the phonological, morphological, and syntactical systems of the language he has acquired.

11. <u>New York City Language Rating Scale</u> - a scale devised to assess the oral proficiency of children in respect to their learning English. It was designed to aid in the screening and placement process of children in the schools and to aid the teacher in diagnosing areas of English language deficiencies or strengths (see Appendix A).

12. <u>Open classroom</u> - an informal environment designed to set the atmosphere in keeping with the concepts of open education.

13. <u>Open education</u> - has been influenced by what is known today about child development and by the progressive education movement in the days of Dewey. It is "a way of thinking about children and learning. It is characterized by openness and trust; by spatial openness of doors and rooms, by openness of time to release and serve children, not to constrain, prescribe, and master them" (Nyquist & Hawes, 1972, p. 11). Stephens (1974) stated "open education is an approach to education that is open to change, to new ideas, to curriculum, to scheduling, to use of space, to honest expressions of feeling between teacher and pupil and between pupil and pupil and open to children's participation in significant decision making in the classroom" (p. 27).

Basic Hypotheses

During preliminary observation by the investigator there was some evidence that continuous peer interaction and manipulation of materials in various learning centers proved to be motivational for active language usage. At least second language acquisition appeared to resemble first language acquisition in a natural context. A field study was decided upon to test the two basic hypotheses which follow:

1. That the language learner would increase his communicative competence in the open classroom environment and thus increase his ability to comprehend in reading. In other words encoding and decoding practices would greatly enhance reading skills and thus broaden the

cognitive base.

2. That the posttest scores would statistically reflect a significant difference in the language competence of second language learners in the open classroom as compared to those in the control group in the traditional classroom.

Significance of the Study

Since the second language learners represent members of minority groups who have been demanding quality integrated education in the United States in order to achieve educationally and economically, this study had significance with respect to how the past ineffectiveness of the schools could be reversed in view of new theories leading to new knowledges.

National and international developments in linguistics, psychology, human development, biology, sociology, and the social sciences in general have been emerging with the onset of the 1970's seeking solutions to problems of man controlling his ever changing environment. These world wide humanitarian movements are challenging educators to seek solutions to problems at the local level. The classroom ought to be a place to develop ways of dealing with difficulties confronting human beings. But, the question is what kind of classroom? The traditional, teacher-dominated classroom has been criticized as ineffective in educating the masses of children.

Educators hold the key to reducing social and emotional barriers confronting minorities. American education, in the author's view, can contribute greatly towards desired changes only if it can focus on the full actualization of man and his ability to shape his environment. Experimentation of new settings in new systems showing real progress in this direction needs to be implemented with proper staff development, continual modification to meet ever changing goals, and the ability to generate support at the local level. The most promising models developed can be initiated and experimentally used until such time it may become operable. Focusing on the development of all men constitutes the recognizable importance of language to the issue of self-actualization. Little research has been conducted until recently on how languages are learned, what it is to generate equality among groups, how to overcome superiority feelings and prejudices, or how to handle social conflict.

Provocative and innovative developments in linguistic theories and child development theories have surfaced to challenge researchers in education. The linguists: psychological, descriptive, historical, sociological, and cultural and offering new insights into reasons why "Johnny can or cannot read," and are bringing their body of knowledge into educational research. The linguists, principally Bloomfield (1933), Fries (1960), and Chomsky (1968), have revolutionized the study of language and have provided significant insights into how language develops. At the same time the psychologists Bruner (1962) and Piaget (1969) have concurrently revolutionized the study of child development. The evolution of child-centered, learning concept-based theories were responsible in some measure for the emergence of new classroom prototypes to accompany these concepts. Implicit in these new ideas is Maslow's (1968) theory of self-actualization. In order to meet the new challenge posed by theory building in sociology and psychology, it has become clear that educators must in tandem be prepared to examine the dynamics of their own classroom models so that they can become uniquely responsive to special educational priorities.

4

New reading programs like Distar, Open Court and a series of programmed materials have not made any significant progress in the public schools as indicated by the continuous decline of reading test scores in New York City. New methods for teaching mathematics, social studies, and science have been instituted into the curriculum. But these new programs for educational development continue to focus on methods, materials, techniques, and procedures. It is necessary to find alternative systems and settings to test educational theories in different structural arrangements. Areas of affective learning are equally as important as the cognitive learning if the "whole child" concept is to be recognized. Since the language learner's advanced expectation of failure may account for his low level of motivation, his disinterest in competitive and challenging academic situations and his eventual drop-out, it may be necessary to center special attention on natural, integrated settings designed to lead him to his maximum potential, i.e., child-centered environments offering freedom of choices, freedom of movement, freedom of interpersonal relationships, and freedom of expression.

Limitations of the Study

This study may well be viewed as a feasibility project mainly because of the limitations in the selection of the subject to be studied. The number of children selected was limited because second language learners rated "C" or "D" on the Language Rating Scale were seldom found in open classrooms and most open classrooms were on the primary level (K-2). The investigation was limited at the outset to fourth grade children who were rated "C" or "D" on the October 1974 census of language learners within the public schools. There were further limitations in scope, materials and procedures, because there are so many variables to consider in the study of language learning. Time was a limiting factor. In retrospect, had a longer period of time been contemplated, much of the research would have been broader in scope.

Methods for analyzing the data were limited because of the sensitivity of the insturment to elicit reliability or validity of the second language learners' true language rating or the instruments to measure the true perceptions of parents or teachers.

Since the number of variables in language research was so extensive, the investigator limited the extrinsic variables influencing the study to:

1. Methods of teaching ESL and the individual teacher's competence were important to this study. The length of time, extent of training and experiences each teacher brought to the particular classroom were analyzed on the basis of a questionnaire.

2. A screening and placement form was used by the investigator to determine age, place of birth, previous schooling, language spoken at home, and number of years child has been in New York City public schools.

3. Cultural values may have some ties in learning another language. Psychological variables as they relate to personality traits and learning successes are important factors. Researchers investigating language acquisition ought to be aware of the social factors which affect teaching, learning, and the use of language. Parent questionnaires and interviews are expected to give some insight into the cultural patterns of the family groups.

Need and Justification for the Study

Generally speaking most teachers are unaware of the principles and practices of teaching English as a second language, even though there is a recognizable need for this training in the public schools. There are both short range and long range needs for the study to awaken the extent of the problem in the immediate classroom and in the broader society. These needs are listed as Educational Needs for the Study and Societal Needs for the Study.

Educational Needs for the Study

1. To become aware of the large number of second language learners rated "C" on the New York City Language Rating Scale who are poor readers, because they did not acquire the English language well enough to achieve at grade level in reading.
2. To note that communicative competence has a positive relationship to socialization and conversation.
3. To realize the importance of psycholinguistics and sociolinguistics in the development of a student's communicative competence.
4. To eliminate the practice of placing children in mentally retarded classes or special schools largely based upon their inability to handle the English language. Deficiencies in second language communication do not necessarily infer cognitive impoverishment.
5. To become aware that for the total integration of the language learner in the life of the school, the socialization process is necessary, including the sharing of variant experiences from diverse cultural backgrounds.
6. To become aware that in the early childhood school grades, the use of concrete materials and greater physical movement provide help to the second language learner. However, in the upper grades fewer concrete materials, more abstractions, less physical mobility and less concern for affective learning handicap natural human development. Research shows that over 85 percent verbal interactions are instituted by a teacher in the traditional class.
7. To be aware of the extent of the language problem in the New York City public schools from their statistics of 1973 showing there are 143,000 students rated "C through F" from 36 foreign countries representing different cultural or linguistic backgrounds.[1]
8. To become aware that second language acquisition is not only a local interest but deeply concerns many nations around the world.

Continuous development of man to reach his complete fulfillment in life within his environment is a basic educational objective that is national and international in scope. Education is not a separate problem but part of a social, economic, and political one all over the world. "While educational strategies are substantially national involving a nation's own sovereign choices, they may at the same time draw ideas from the international context and benefit from useful examples contained in the wealth of educational experiences in all countries" (Faure, Felipe, Kaddoura, Lopez, Petrovsky, Rahnema, & Ward, 1972, p. 178).

Expanding education to meet the needs of individuals and societies has become a reality as witnessed by the organization of UNESCO within the United Nations concerned for human needs,

Afghanistan[1]	Egypt	Israel	Philippines
Bolivia	El Salvador	Italy	Poland
Brazil	France	Japan	Puerto Rico
Chile	Greece	Korea	Santo Domingo
Columbia	Guatemala	Liberia	Spain
Costa Rica	Haiti	Mexico	St. Maarten
Cuba	Hong Kong	Nicaragua	Taiwan (Republic of China)
Dominican Republic	India	Pakistan	Turkey
Ecuador	Iran	Peru	Venezuela

International Organization for the Study of Group Tensions, and the Ford Foundation offering large grants to language development programs in various parts of the world. Because the concept of "one world" is enfluencing national and international policies, it is not uncommon to find world-wide committees and conferences convening to seek solutions to common problems.

Linguists and second language teachers from countries across the land can select those research ideas and thoughts presented in studies leading to possible solutions to problems affecting their specific situations. The list of societal needs reflects similar concerns of countries in Africa, Asia, South America and North America.

Societal Needs for the Study

1. To reverse the process that shows language learners become drop-outs or push-outs because the schools did not meet their educational needs.
2. To take a more critical look at the underlying causes of minority delinquency. Is educational failure increasing the vulnerability to antisocial behavior?
3. To understand the uniqueness and diversity of life and learn the best of all cultures.
4. To overcome the obstacles of prejudicial values, attitudes, and ignorance through widening social interaction in the school years.
5. To understand that planned change is necessary to progress especially in regards to teaching.
6. To reduce the degree of tensions between the larger society in conflict with the language learning minority through efforts at analyzing the causes of human conflict and methods for prevention or treatment of the initial causes.
7. To become aware of the need to integrate knowledge from the other disciplinary studies that have practical classroom adaptation.
8. To understand that world problems are in need of human resources including those who are being wasted in the schools.
9. To become aware that future trends towards a more humanistic approach to life are challenging all disciplines.
10. To become involved in organizations like TESOL which is international, national and local in scope. This organization has been moving in an interdisciplinary direction to prepare people to communicate competently in languages so essential to human understanding.
11. To become involved in organizations such as the International Council on Education for Teaching and the International Organization for the Study of Group Tensions. The latter provides a quarterly journal, lectures, seminars and workshops for groups to study conflict and violence in human relations. This service is provided anywhere in the United States and overseas (Gittler, 1974).

Organization of the Study

This study is divided into five chapters. Chapter I included the statement of the problem, the key concepts, the basic hypotheses, the significance of the study, limitations of the study, need and justification for the study including short range educational needs and long range societal needs. Chapter II included a review of selected, related literature divided into four parts, areas of specialties which supported and influenced the growth of English as a second language up to 1970; child development and open education theories that contributed to new theories in teaching English as a second language; recent studies in second language acquisition influenced by the child development theories; and future perspectives in education. Chapter III described the subjects, materials, and procedures used in conducting the study and collecting the data. Chapter IV reported the findings and a comparative analysis and synthesis of the open and traditional classroom environments. The last chapter (V) presented the summary, conclusions, and recommendations of the research study.

CHAPTER II

REVIEW OF THE RELATED LITERATURE

Introduction

For purposes of clarity of presentation, this chapter presented an overview of the related literature and research focusing on: (1) the literature related to the contributions made by the specialists toward the growth of English as a second language; (2) child development and the concept of open education; (3) more recent studies in second language acquisition influenced by child development theories; and (4) future perspectives in education.

Note on Inclusion Criteria

The emergence of new philosophical concepts, centered around child development, necessitated reviewing studies and literature across many disparate disciplines. The author's interest in the interdisciplinary approach to solving educational problems led to a search for materials focusing on the cognitive, affective, emotional, social, and linguistic development of children. Emphasis was placed on reviewing those innovative approaches which have reflected successes in the development of communicative competence programs for second language learners.

Part I: The Literature Related to the Contributions Made by the Specialists Toward the Growth of English as a Second Language

Because of the total dependence on and the need for language, many studies across disciplines have contributed to second language teaching in the past and in the present. It is expected that these disciplines will contribute even more in the future. Noted and described in this section are the contributions having come forward from the philosophers, anthropologists, linguists, psychologists, speech specialists, sociologists, and human relations experts.

Contributions from Philosophers

In tracing the history of educational philosophies, it has become apparent in view of the traditional, contemporary classroom that those teaching methods and procedures used in the traditional classroom are historically observable in Aristotle's "realism" and Plato's "idealism." These philosophers placed the teacher as the all authoritative figure in the classroom and the school as the perpetuator of contemporary morals and values. The Aristotelian and Platonic doctrines have done much to influence the course in history of American education which demands systematic and critical review at this time. The criticism launched against these philosophies derived largely from the fact that they ignore the sensorimotor needs of the individual, set unobtainable goals, overlook the possibility of error, cannot deal with failure, and deemphasize the cultural and linguistic experiences children bring with them to the classroom. Education in the days of Aristotle and

Plato was for the privileged few and remained that way for centuries. However, education today has become one of the leading national priorities in America, in Europe and in the developing countries of the Third World people. UNESCO of the United Nations has joined nations to discuss the prevailing theme of education with an international thrust. In Harrap, England, in 1972 there was a conference to exchange ideas and plan strategies for international education. The report from the International Commission on the Development of Education was published in a book written by Faure et al. (1972) which best traced the history of education from Aristotle and Plato to the present.

The history of education and its progress was closely tied to progress in economics first and then to the social and political areas. The more skills were needed the more trained people were necessary to perform these skills. Man first had to learn to adapt to his environment or to conquer it. Learning how to survive required learning which is a human biological ability. Education in a primitive society was family oriented and revolved around learning from parents or listening to tales passed down from older folks. Knowledge was taken from the environment. African societies, for example, learned by living and doing. Oral education "involved direct contact with things and people" (Faure et al., 1972, p. 6). Books gradually replaced the direct method of oral learning.

Education in Asia was similar to education in Africa. In classical Greece and Rome education was primarily for the elite and emphasis was on teaching philosophy and religion. Ancient Western societies and those of the middle ages confined education to the aristocrats. "Mediaeval education was essentially a response to the conditions of feudal society as well as to religious ideas" (p. 8). "The Muslims world was among the first to recommend the ideas of lifelong education, exhorting Muslims to educate themselves 'from the cradle to the grave'" (p. 8). The Arab and Muslim world deserved recognition for "flourishing culture which extended through Asia, Africa, and to Europe" (p. 9). Although some modern educational philosophies can be traced back to the ancient past, societies on the whole were slow to evolve and education remained static.

The invention of the printing press made books available to the masses who had not been exposed to education before. This invention and the industrial revolution popularized education in many countries around the world including those that were colonized. The concept of compulsory education came into being, but emphasis was still on class and social order. Education continued to be slow in making any significant philosophical changes until World War II. Emphasis on the natural sciences at this time was responsible for the advancement of technology and the deemphasis on the human sciences. Traditionalism in American education remained unchallenged until James (1909) and Dewey (1936) aimed at placing meaning to truth in practical social situations. Theoretically the individual became responsible for his own learning through problem solving. Brameld (1941) went a step further in believing philosophy was a tool that should help build a more informed society and perhaps a better culture. Brameld and other reconstructionists felt schools should be, therefore, culture oriented. These seemingly modern concepts remained mostly isolated studies and never reached the implementation stage. It was not until the third world peoples' liberation movements all over the world followed by the Civil Rights movement in America in the 1950's and 60's demanding equal opportunities to attain educationally that American education received a jolt. America was unprepared to meet the educational demands having patterned her educational philosophies from Western European philosophers and reformers. However, recently governments at the city, state, and federal levels have been either independently or collectively spending large sums of money on educational research to advance democratic principles within educational reform; thus educators are beginning to take their place in the research world.

Contributions from Anthropologists

Cultural and social anthropologists have long been interested in men and his environment. They were perhaps the first group to trace languages to people within their own environment. Boas (1940), a most distinguished anthropologist, studied the American Indians and their language. He concluded that language, as part of culture, could not be fully understood unless one is in the position to appreciate that language and understand the culture surrounding that language.

Boas (1911), Sapir (1949), and Whorf (1956), in the course of their field experiments with informants, described the spoken language and then the written language of many Northwestern and Southwestern American Indians including the Sioux and the Navajo nations. These social scientists attempted to describe specific structural aspects of language, most notably the phonology of language. Their independent studies led to the introduction of descriptive linguistics (attempts to describe phonology, morphology, and syntax of language) and comparative linguistics (attempt to compare two languages and the difficulties one language speaker might expect to encounter when beginning to learn another language).

Contributions from Linguists

After World War II, the study of traditional or classical grammer with its emphasis on learning rules for parts of speech was challenged by the many linguists who strongly rejected the memorization of rules which were molded after a dead language - Latin, and which did not apply to spoken language which constantly changes in structure, form and function. Bloomfield (1951) was among the prominent linguists to renounce the traditional grammar in favor of descriptive linguistics describing how living languages are actually used. While Bloomfield (1951), Sapir (1921, 1949), Trager and Smith (1965) developed studies decoding the phonological aspects of language, Palmer in England (1940) followed by Fries (1952) in America were not only interested in phonology but in analyzing syntactic relationships in sentences in respect to word forms (inflections of function words) and of word order. The Merrill Linguistic Reader (1966) written under the direction of Fries (1963) reflected Fries' linguistic concerns in language development. Chomsky (1957) believed that given a structure as a grammatical pattern that structure can be changed through transformation rules to generate many sentences. Chomsky's contributions have been most impressive and important to the study of language. He has been instrumental in bringing grammar back to language teaching.

Chomsky opposed the behaviorists like Skinner. He theorized that language is not just a set of habits as scientific evidence in testing animal communication. Human beings are different from animals and should be recognized as such by science and government. In Lyon's (1970) book Chomsky claimed "that the principles underlying the structure of language are so specific and so highly articulated that they must be regarded as being biologically determined," that is to say, as constituting part of what we call "human nature" and as being genetically transmitted from parents to their children. Chomsky's theory of transformational grammar has been one of the first attempts to systematically describe and explain the structure of human language as one part of a complex human behavior, which is "common to all members of the species, regardless of their race or class and their undoubted differences in intellect, personality, and physical attributes" (p. 8).

Lyons, in his study of modern linguists and Chomsky's input in particular, distinguished the differences between traditional grammar and linguistics. One major characteristic of modern linguistics that differs from traditional grammar "is its autonomy or independence of other disciplines" (p. 12). This has been explained as taking "a fresh and objective look at language without prior commitment to traditional ideas and without necessarily adopting the same point of view of philosophers, psychologists, literary critics, or representatives of other disciplines" (p. 13). Traditional grammar like Western culture, in general, grew out of Greek philosophical doctrines which gave much attention to written language as the model for the spoken language. Modern linguists, on the contrary, view speech as primary to any form of language.

Another characteristic of human language is "the capacity that all native speakers of a language have to produce and understand an indefinitely large number of sentences that they have never heard before and they may indeed never have been uttered before by anyone" (p. 21). The interrelatedness of syntax, semantics, and phonology is believed by the modern linguists to account for a native speaker's ability to produce and understand an indefinite number of sentences. Traditional grammarians had set up prescriptive rules of grammar to be followed by users of the language.

In Chomsky's later works, Aspects of Theory of Syntax (1965), Cortesian Linguistics (1966), and Language and Mind (1968) he had moved away from the autonomy of linguistics to linguistics as a branch of psychology. Chomsky suggested linguists move from the investigation of language to the use of language, from linguistic competence to linguistic performances. Chomsky added that the speaker's intuitions (his mental representation of grammar of the language) are the true objects of description. As a result of Chomsky's transformational rules, psychologists have been testing the validity of these transformations with cognitive development. It has been shown that "active sentences could be remembered more easily than passive sentences, and affirmative sentences more easily than negative sentences" (Lyons, 1970, p. 104). Chomsky also believed that linguists can make an important contribution to the study of the human mind in which he favored the rationalists' philosophy of reason over the impiricists. According to the former group, reason is the sole source of human knowledge, while the latter group believed all knowledge is derived from experiences. It was this thinking that led Chomsky to hold that "it is the central purpose of linguistics to construct a deductive theory of the structure of human language that is at once sufficiently general to apply to all languages...or linguistics should determine the universal and essential properties of human language" (Lyons, 1970, pp. 110-111).

Chomsky's views on the universality of language are based upon physiological and psychological characteristics of the human being. All languages fulfill a similar range of functions as making statements, asking questions, issuing commands, changing tenses, and making plurals.

Chomsky maintains that it is only by assuming that the
child is born with a knowledge of the highly restrictive
principles of universal grammar and the predisposition
to make use of them in analyzing the utterances he hears
about him, that we can make any sense of the process of
language learning. (Lyons, 1970, p. 118)

Chomsky's ideas have influenced a number of different disciplines
but have also inspired many linguists and English as a second language
educators to study certain aspects of language considered "universal"
in seeking to formulate a universal grammar.

Pike (1967) was the first to introduce the tagmemic theory of
linguistics which states that language data are patterned behavior within a patterned context. The suffix "emic" means a distinctive slot.
A structural meaning is identified with that slot. Thus word form and
function are combined to bring meaning to an utterance. Dictionaries
and spellers are tagmemic in nature. The dictionary gives several
meanings of the same word so that one can select the appropriate
meaning to be used according to its place in a sentence. The speller,
for example, will determine which "bare, bear" will be used in a sentence. The linguists brought to the educators an awareness of the
how's, why's, and what's of language learning and an appreciation of
the intricacies of human language in regional and geographic context.
They have sparked considerable interest in second language learning,
bilingual education, and dialectal differences in languages.

In the past two decades awareness in new frontiers, centered
around language learning, persuaded linguists to broaden their scope.
Lado (1961) in Linguistic Across Cultures focused on new dimensions in
learning a second language, i.e., recognition of the cultural, philosophical, sociological, and psychological theoretical components of
linguistics. Structural linguists, who insisted that grammatical
definitions must be based on form and function rather than real or
presumed meaning, were called to revise materials for language teaching
in high school and to clarify systems or methods for teaching languages
in Europe and in America. It was during this time that interest in
language learning was generated as organizations in America began to
grow in membership - The Institute of Modern Languages, Foreign
Language Association, Center for Applied Linguistics, Teachers to
Speakers of Other Languages, and the Association of Teachers of English
as a Second Language. Each of these organizations publish journals
disseminating valuable research information to their constituents.

Contributions from Psychologists

Psychologists and their learning theories have done much to shape
the course of education. Hilgard (1956), Pavlov (1927), Skinner (1956),
and Thorndike (1932), cited in Bugelski (1964) applied their laws of
learning to the theory of second language learning. Skinner and Hull
(1943), known as associationists as well as behaviorists, both advanced
the concept that since second language acquisition was learning a new
set of habits, it meant learning took place through the method of
stimulus and response or rewarding the learning or reinforcing the
learnings. Oral drills and exercises requiring constant repetition
(aural-oral method) were devised by early linguistis to teach English
as a second language based on these theories. The aural-oral method
was used by the Army Language School to speed up learning a foreign
language through listening to tapes and then mimicking what was heard.

Thorndike explained learning as a trial and error activity with successful attempts reinforced by satisfying consequences. Although this focus might have applied to animals, it did not apply to humans. Lado (1964) claimed the "language learning could not be understood through trial and error, association, gestalt, or overt behavior alone ...it involves simultaneously the widest range in human acitivity" (p. 35).

Pavlov's conditioned reflexes did not apply well to language learning except in "an arbitrary connection between a word and its meaning" (Lado, 1964, p. 36). Thorndike's laws of learning applied only in a limited way to the process of language learning, becuase they were stated in very general terms. Because of the complexity of languages, language learning theories needed special attention and special treatment which is currently being researched.

Psychologists are now discovering new dimensions in the nature of language learning compelling language teachers to develop new approaches to their teaching. The old stimulus-response, audio-lingual, and pattern practice drills are not in keeping with more humanistic approaches focusing on child-centered communication rather than linguistic manipulation.

Contributions from Speech Specialists

Speech specialists Reed (1952) and Thomas (1958) were primarily interested in the motor aspects of speech production. They concentrated on intonation patterns and phonological sounds to help language learners articulate better and attain social acceptance within their peer environment. They pointed up the formation of the tongue, teeth, lip, gum, and mouth in writing the phonetics of the language as it is spoken by the educated in any particular environment. Their contribution to English as a second language is mainly in helping teachers analyze what is heard in spoken language and considered "good speech." Because this researcher sees a relationship between organization of articulation skills and improvement in reading, the contributions by the speech specialists deserve attention.

Contributions from Sociologists

Very little was contributed to the area of second language learning from sociologists before 1970 except to gather statistics and discuss problems of the Puerto Rican migration movement. At the local level many organizations were formed to help orientate the migrant to American ways. Other organizations were formed to help integrate the newcomer into American society (The Welfare Council in New York City and in Chicago, the National Conference on Social Welfare). Senior (1961) wrote about the many local governmental, religious, business, labor, and educational agencies that were formed in the 1960's to welcome, guide and counsel newcomers in the difficulties of establishing themselves. About the same time literature reflecting life in Puerto Rico and on to the United States became available. Exchange programs were instituted between Puerto Rico and the United States to help bridge gaps in the understanding of cultural differences of the latest new arrival who had settled in cities along the Atlantic coast. The social revolution had its roots during these days when America found itself in a dilemma because society was unprepared for and incapable of solving the pressing problem of migration. Local educational systems formed human relations committees to handle the misunderstandings that had

14

developed in socialization.

Contributions from Human Relations Specialists

The human relations specialists, namely Kilpatrick (1949) from Chicago, the Commission on Human Relations in New York and New York City Board of Education, were seeking ways to encourage individuals to engage in dialogues as a method of understanding social differences. These specialists had often been called in as mediators or third party interventionalists when group tensions were at a high level or when social conflict was imminent. Encounter groups, "T" groups and other similar groups have been widely engaged in interaction since the 1960's. Educators in New York City have been required to take a course in human relations in hope that principles of such courses would relate in some measure to the daily school curriculum. It was also hoped that the principles of democracy would be infused in American education as a result of the human relations awareness.

In spite of the fact that there has been an array of impressive scholars contributing to education, second language acquisition was not reaching the needs of the language learner or his teacher. However, other disciplines, e.g., biology, education, and social science are offering further insights into the study of language and its natural development.

Part II: Child Development and the Concept of Open Education

Recent movements of new learning theories have changed educational focus to what education is all about, a continuous process of learning, an accumulation of knowledge, a mastery of skills in which language represents the most important aspect. When children are engaged in lively experiences, they are achieving meaningful knowledges, and the more physical, social and emotional involvement they have with life's experiences within their environment, the more opportunities for developing their own cognitive competencies. James (1909) and Dewey (1936), outstanding experimentalists, were largely responsible for this focus on the process of academic achievement. These two philosophers based their theories primarily on the same premise as the ancient Africans (see p. 19) that man learns by "doing" and that his actions have practical consequences in his own life. However, it was not until recently that the progressive movement led by Dewey and continued by Heidegger and Kant (1967) witnessed revival in America.

The existentialist movement which began during World War I and experienced a revival after World War II is making significant impact on educational theories. The shift was from prescribed curriculum imparted to children to the describing of curriculum that develops in the process of acquiring knowledge. The term existentialism grew out of man's search for meaning to his existence and his ability to perceive himself within his environment. Frequently used hyphenated terms as "self-awareness, self-esteem, self-discipline, self-image, self-worth and self-motivation" are an outgrowth of man's desire to come to grips with "self" in making life's choices. Maslow's (1970) hierarchy of basic human needs is representative of this new concern. Maslow formulated a theory of human motivation based upon basic human needs unlike traditional theories which grew out of animal studies. According to Maslow, all humans have
1. physiological needs
2. safety needs

3. love needs
   4. esteem needs
   5. self-actualization needs.
He rejected traditional learning theories in favor of more human-centered
theories.

   Scientists using a more open, clinical research approach in
studying total human development are feeding their body of knowledges
in a concerted effort to seek solutions to common problems. Researchers
in education are looking at a galaxy of concerns patterning human development and ways in which such development can shape human potential.
Their search leads to the inevitable biological and psychological
maturation of children within a socio-cultural environment. It is within this environment that attention is being focused on language learning.

   In 1965 Winnicott, in his study of the emotional development of
children, discussed the "function of the environment which facilitates
the maturational processes. Environment provision must be 'good'
enough if maturation is to become a fact in the case of any one child"
(p. 206). "Maturation of the human being is a term that implies not
only personal growth but also socialization" (p. 83). Winnicott was
one of the first to theorize that "the capacity to communicate is
closely bound up with relating to objects" (p. 179). He also observed
that "behind a child's maladjustment is always a failure of the
environment to adjust to the child's absolute needs at a time of
relative dependence" (p. 207). He further stated that maturation starts
with the nurturing process at home and continues along in society outside of the home. The school like the home can offer a facilitating
environment for growth to take place. Chomsky (1965), also implied in
his studies that language requires definite active environmental
conditions during the period of maturation.

   Ryan, cited in Richard's (1974) Early Language Development, described studies made by Brown and Bellugi in 1964 in which they observed
that "mothers frequently responded to their child's utterance by
'expanding' it - that is, by reproducing it and also adding something
to it, or otherwise changing it" (p. 199). Adults also modify their
speech towards children in the direction of greater distinctiveness,
"slowness, and simplicity...mostly used short and grammatically correct
sentences when speaking to children" (p. 200). Ryan claimed such
findings emphasize how mothers provide linguistic input for the child
and "early language development thus appears to take place in a context that provides a child with frequent interpretations of his
utterances" (p. 200). The author cited a study by Weir in 1966 where
linguists could distinguish babbling sounds of 4-6 month infants of
Chinese and American parents which reflected some features of the
language spoken at home. "Conditioning studies of 3 month old infants
suggest that the discriminatory capacity for distinguishing various
speech sounds is present from a very early age. It therefore appears
long before parents think they can recognize familiar sounds in the
vocalizations of children, the sounds made do in fact bear some resem-
blance to the native language" (Eimas et al., 1971, pp. 200-201).
She concluded that a child has learned something general about speech
long before he starts to imitate from adults.

   Studies like those just mentioned gave rise to the notion that
the reason a child cannot hear or produce certain phonemes not in his
own language is primarily, because the phonemes of his native language
are what is heard and practiced from the start of his language development. It is within the child's capacity to make sounds which later
become speech sounds in language development. As he practices the

sounds of his own native language, all other sounds not being heard or practiced are ignored. In second language learning, phonological differences between languages have been one of the major concerns of second language teachers, suggesting that perhaps second language learners, like first language learners, need to hear and practice the speech sounds of the target language for a period of time before semantics enter.

Ryan, in her own observations of children in the process of acquiring their first language, provided a framework of a holistic view for an empirical analysis and description of the communication skills that a child acquires during the first two years combining his social environment and his bilogical structure. Her observations led her to be critical of psycholinguists, Cazden (1968) and McNeill (1966, 1970) and others who neglected the presyntactic stage of language development when concentrating on mastery of grammar to the neglect of communicative competence - "Communication...includes all interaction and is analyzed in terms of consequences and effects" (p. 210). Ryan's philosophical conclusion is that acquiring a language in itself constitutes a form of socialization where dialogues with others are social rather than individual. "Any analysis of human communication must include a description of the structure of intersubjectivity between participants in a dialogue" (p. 211). She suggested further studies are needed in the areas of communicative language, dialogues, verbal and nonverbal, in reciprocal interchanges made between children and adults and/or children and children. Her studies have implications for all teachers who shape the social environment in the classroom as an extension of the home.

Sharing some of the same holistic views resulting from their extensive studies in child development and the competent child are Kaban and Shapiro (1975), Mussen, Conger, and Kagan (1969), White, and Whiting and Whiting (1974). Their studies have superceded Piaget who has reached a position of pre-eminence in child development.

Piaget perceived language as a means of knowing and thinking and not something that is to be studied. Therefore, according to Piaget, language is learned not necessarily through a process of operant reinforcement but through exposure to words in context. "Piaget sees language as simply one facet of cognitive development, providing an economical means of representing reality" (Ryan, 1974, p. 191). Piaget (1969) perceived language developing in coordination with sensori-motor schemes which are actively built up during the first months of life. He has contributed insightful information to curriculum researchers who are presently developing Piagetian tasks to coincide with his projected concepts. He has attracted linguists (in Part III) who are looking at language learning theories differently. Piaget (1969) applied "knowing" to language postulating that knowing when applied to language is more than just knowing the language; it is also having ideas to express in that language. Bruner (1966) and Gattegno (1971) defined "knowing" in more general terms as dependent upon
1. awareness of abstractions
2. awareness of similarities and differences
3. awareness of functions and interactive relationships.
These are recognizable goals set by those educators now becoming aware of the methods they are using and the materials they have selected to obtain the desired objectives.

In 1961 Bruner added impressive principles to learning theories when he stated "The child comes to manipulate his environment more actively and achieve his gratification from coping with problems"(p.166).

Furthermore "the very attitudes and activities that characterize 'figuring out' or discovering things for oneself also seems to have the effect of making material more readily accessible in memory" (p. 168). Thus the problem-solving process and the discovery, explor- atory process aroused interest among those educators looking for posi- tive improvements in educating children. In 1966 Bruner explored another important concept of "intrinsic" motives for learning which almost all children possess. "Curiosity is almost a prototype of the intrinsic move" (p. 33). The drive to achieve competence is also an intrinsic motive that was well expressed by White in 1959 but gained recognition in 1974. White, very aptly stated the following:

> According to Webster, competence means fitness or ability, and the suggested synonyms include capability, capacity, efficiency, proficiency, and skill. It is therefore a suitable word to describe such things as grasping and exploring, crawling and walking, attention and perception, all of which promote an effective - a competent - inter- action with environment. It is true, of course, that maturation plays a part in all these development, but this part is heavily overshadowed by learning in all the more complex accomplishments like speech or skilled manipulation. I shall argue that it is necessary to make competence a motivational concept; there is competence motivation as well as competence in its more familiar sense of achieved capacity. The behavior that leads to the building up of effective grasping, handling, and letting go of objects, to take one example, is not random behavior that is produced by an overflow of energy. It is directed, selective, and persistent, and it continues not because it serves primary drives, which indeed it cannot serve until it is almost perfect, but because it satisfies an intrinsic need to deal with the environment. (p. 35)

Maslow (1968) added the concept of "freedom of choice" to the learning process. He noted that safety needs of a child are prepotent to growth needs. When a child feels safe enough, he will use his natural curiosity to make choices for himself. In 1972 he reemphasized the idea of a child making choices in this quotation: "Each bit of active experiencing is an opportunity toward finding out what he likes or dislikes, and more and more what he wants to make out of himself. It is an essential part of his progress toward the stage of maturity and self direction" (p. 46).

> The results of active experiencing can be summarized approximately in the following way. There is physical, emotional, and intellectual self-involvement; there is a recognition and further exploration of one's abilities; there is initiation of activity or creativeness; there is finding out one's own pace and rhythm and the assumption of enough of a task for one's abilities at that particular time, which would include the avoidance of taking on too much; there is gain in which one can apply to other enterprises, and there is an opportunity each time that one has an active part in something, no matter how small, to find out more and more what one is interested in. (p. 46)

Lenneberg, an eminent biological scholar, in 1967 published Biological Foundations of Language in which he conceptualized that roots of social communication of experience and intention are well established at birth. Through the social process a three year old indicates competence in language understanding more than he can express orally. His language acquisition has been completed, since most of the basic grammatical structures used by adults are present in the child's language, and he can recognize and deal with syntactic structure of sentences whose meanings are new or unclear to him. Refinements in syntax will come about through his cognitive development. In 1964 Lenneberg continued to support his own theory that "interaction between the environmental input and maturation are important in language development" (p. 631). Working closely with linguists, particularly Chomsky, psychologists and other biologists, Lenneberg has contributed valuable information needed for continued research in language acquisition. He observed early signs of communication in babies from the fetal stage on to maturity. He noticed that the mouth opening and tongue retraction during the fetal stage preceded lip pursing and tongue protracting and that "movement and expressions of the mouth and tongue occur at the same time as reach and grasp" (p. 575). He contended that this is a sign of babies passing comments on their acts to other persons. In his discussion of "Language and the Brain," he reviewed many studies in progress linking social communication and language development. He concluded, as did Ryan (1974), that

> roots of social communication of experience and intention
> are well established at birth. Richards and Trevarthen in
> Bruner's laboratory at the Center for Cognitive Studies at
> Harvard discovered young infants categorize unliving physical
> objects as different from living intelligent objects like
> their mother and behave quite differently to these two
> kinds of things. (Lenneberg, 1974, p. 579)

He applied his findings to the understanding of language and its developmental stages.

> What has been learned is that the social context of
> intellectual development is established genetically
> at the start of the infant's life. (p. 582)

> With regard to imitation, these young babies lead their
> mothers into elaborate imitation of their more emotional
> expressions and only rarely have the infants been observed
> to imitate the mother. (p. 582)

> Piaget (1962) has found that the best behaviors to study
> for imitation are hand movements, mouth and tongue move-
> ments, and head movements, all of which are important in
> communication. (p. 582)

> From the start, efforts to speak, while especially con-
> strained to a context of communication, are coupled with
> efforts to see or to use objects. (p. 584)

> Newborn human beings show, in rudimentary form many of
> the remarkable behaviors of adult intelligence, including
> a form of speech as a means of communication. (p. 584)

Speech has evolved out of the need for communication of intention and experience between beings of like psychological organization, with the same manner and cadence of attending to the events in the common environment. (p. 585)

If the perceptual system should develop in such a way as to make it possible to understand only one type of sentence form, then only such grammars could develop that conform to those perceptual abilities and constraints. It is conceivable, however, that the separate system of grammatical knowledge within the child is powerful enough to include rules that would generate sentences that exceed the perceptual capacities of the child. (p. 586)

One linguistic universal is the predicate relationship between a noun and verb...Linguists must isolate those universal aspects of language structure (competence) that do not simply follow from functional properties of the human organism. (p. 586)

At age two, a child has a stereotyped way of interpreting sentences. A noun followed by a verb becomes an actor-action sequence such as:
1. The cow kissed the horse. (understood by the child)
2. The horse is kissed by the cow. (not understood)
3. It is the horse that the cow kissed. (understood because the child picks out the actor-action, cow kisses) (pp. 586-587)
At the age of four, a more general strategy for sentence analysis develops. The structural rule is "consider the first noun that occurs in a sequence as the actor" (p. 587). In this case, sentences of type 1 are correctly interpreted but not sentences of type 2 or 3.

Bever (1971) reported his study with children 2-1/2 to 5 years old, the ages when ear preference develops. The author discovered that understanding of sentences is closely tied to ear preference rather than general auditory processing. In another study with bilingual children, Bever noticed children with intermediate mastery, their second language, performed worse on sentences 2 and 3 and better on 1 than children with a beginning mastery. The author concluded that ear preference had not yet developed if the input was English, and therefore ear preference may be related to stages of development in learning a new language. From this he deduced that children should be given special training using one ear with hopes of developing advanced strategy of sentence interpretation.

Chomsky's (1965) generative grammar theory is helping the biologist of today in some way to define the meaning of complexity in the structure of sentences. Lenneberg (1974) concluded that the development of language involves structural changes in the brain and that language moves from an undifferentiated stage to a degree of specialization and differentiation.

Recently there has been a continuum of acceptance of Lenneberg's theories by other scientists studying cognition and the brain. Hart (1974) was critical of the tradtional schools that have neglected the brain in the learning process even though it has been established scientifically that "The brain is specifically designed as speech. The brain works logically and sequentially only under protest. The brain hungers for input." Delgado (1975), cited in Saturday Review, believes man can direct his own evolution, because his brain as well as his culture can be modified.

The new philosophical concepts of child development exacted from many disciplines are being scientifically observed across the country. Rogers (1972) best defined and discussed significant elements in the experiential learning process. He identified a new set of assumptions essential to the purpose of learning in a constantly changing world.

1. Human beings have a natural potentiality for learning.

2. Significant learning takes place when the subject matter is perceived by the student as having relevance for his own purposes.

3. Much significant learning is acquired through doing.

4. Learning is facilitated when the student participates responsibly in the learning process.

5. Self-initiated learning involving the whole person of the learner - feelings as well as intellect - is most pervasive and lasting.

6. Creativity in learning is best facilitated when self-criticism and self-evaluation are primary and evaluation by others is secondary in importance.

7. The most socially useful learning in the modern world is the learning of the process of learning, a continuing openness to experience, an incorporation into oneself of the process of change. (pp. 278-279)

As a psychologist, Rogers' set of assumptions points out basic human needs motivating man to fulfill himself. In Maslow's (1970) theory of motivation, he placed self-actualization as the ultimate of human needs. He theorized that thwarting of these needs produces feelings of inferiority or helplessness. This researcher sees the importance of Maslow's theory for educators. Those language learners who have not succeeded in school have become the dropouts in society having developed feelings of helplessness. However, more and more attention to this central importance of self-fulfillment have been evidenced by the bilingual movement, the open classroom movement, and the rise of alternative schools.

In order to attain the principles set down by psychologists, educators saw the need to set new environments to make these new principles possible and operational. Barth (1972), Blitz and Silberman (1973), Bremer and Bremer (1972), Kohl (1969), Myquist and Hawes (1972), Silberman, Allender, and Yanoff (1972), Stephens (1974), and Weber (1971) have researched the implementation of the new learning theories into an open education environment often referred to in New York City as the open classroom. These specialists have not only introduced the changing educational assumptions but offer concrete suggestions to educators on how to recognize the problems of managing time and space, discipline, the changing role of the teacher, the process of individualization, and the use of an abundance of learning materials.

Much of the literature on child development leads to the concept of open education and how it differs instructionally and structurally from the more traditional education. What appears to be observable differences between the two educational philosophies have been outlined by the recent literature on child development. It is believed that the open classroom is more likely to exhibit the following criteria:

1. The atmosphere in the classroom is pupil centered and learning centered where pupils have choices in carrying out their plan of study, where learning combines the emotional, physical, and intellectual nature of each child, and where the child pursues his own happiness with pride, self-assurance, dignity, and self-esteem.

2. Problem solving is the road to learning as the child acts independently and responsibly for his own learning. He is freer to

explore, discover and create.

3. The room arrangement reflects many active learning centers with an enthusiasm for doing and a respect for much social interaction.

4. Materials are out of closets and in constant use to satisfy the child's natural curiosity and need to manipulate objects.

5. Shared experiences become the basis for communication.

6. Individual differences are acknowledged and encouraged.

7. There is interdisciplinary approach to children's learning.

8. Creativity is encouraged challenging the intellect both cognitively and affectively.

Advocates of the modern theories have been critical of the traditional classroom which has been viewed as the classroom that has a prescribed curriculum centered around learning the three R's, memorizing facts from history and geography, being obedient and honest through the system of punishment and reward, competing with peers for grades and learning morality and values from the teacher. It is also characterized as having homogeneous ability grouping with the teacher at the center of the class lecturing information children are expected to memorize without any real purpose. The general pedagogical principle is: "This is what you have to do; this is how you have to do it; do it and I will mark it to see if you have done it correctly; then I will reward or punish you accordingly" (Silberman, 1973, p. 67).

Some of the authors discussed specifically how language and reading develop naturally in an open classroom. Williams' paper on "Reading in the Informal Classroom" in Nyquist and Hawes (1972) claimed that reading is a basic attitude and a skill. In a free atmosphere children become convinced that books are sources of pleasure, mines of information, vital links between them and their extending curiosity. Now they want to master them for their own purposes and pleasures. The importance of oral speech as the foundation of language and of reading cannot be over-emphasized (pp. 137-145). It becomes necessary for the teacher to make a wise selection of reading materials - books, games, picture cards, and flash cards. Emphasis should be placed on practicing a skill with the teacher or with a peer. All of these steps are essential to the basic theme of preparing second language learners for success in reading in English. Bremer and Bremer (1972), in consonance with the linguists, stressed the communication process as a listening-speaking phenomenon. Second language learners need to listen to associate words with objects, to imitate and to practice these words. The two authors associated languages with a "happening," a sharing between student to student, a development of social skills, and acitivity involving listening and speaking (pp. 40-41).

Silberman supported the scientific approach to learning expressed by the advocates of the experimental method of research. He applied the concept to learning subject matter in the open classroom. He strongly contended that reading is not just a subject, but it permeates a child's entire life. The second language learners' chances to rehearse language while relating to animals, puppets, and drama are maximized in an open classroom environment. Silberman also stated that the child learning English as a second language will have a long period of intake and interaction. He must enjoy the sound of the language, patterns, and intonation of words through hearing them. "The demand for production seems to inhibit intake and narrow synthesizing of the forms of a new language" (p. 543). He defined reading in the following way. "Reading is an extension of language development. Language is grounded in and develops out of personal experiences enabling individuals to codify, clarify, and extend his

22

understanding of objects, situations, and relationships" (p. 539).

The key to any open classroom is the facilitating environment with a facilitating teacher. The school environment becomes an extension of the home and the teacher's role resembles the mother figure in the home. Within this setting the possibility for peer tutoring is maximized.

Before open education became a popular concept, Williams (cited in Braun, 1971) stated in his article "The Pre-Adolescent Boys and Girls," the nine and ten year old child is socially, emotionally, intellectually, and physically capable of helping each other and needs the opportunity to grow and appreciate people of other cultures, creed, and race who need help. In another of his papers, "Helping the Bilingual Child" (1964), he recommended keeping the bilingual child close to his English speaking peers to give him language experiences which are meaningful in solving problems children generally meet daily in their play, work and conversing. Chavez (1956) earlier contended "a second language can become a common denominator - a basis where better understanding of cultural differences prevails among children" (p. 478).

In 1971 Bremer and von Moschzisher wrote a book on the Parkway Program that developed in Philadelphia in February 1969. "The fundamental contention of this book and the Parkway Program is that no changes in an educational system will be of any significance unless the social organization of education is totally changed, that is, unless the system itself is changed" (p. 11). The Parkway Program was designed to implement the new theories in human development. It opened primarily for high school students and gained favorable publicity. The Gamma Community of the Parkway Program was opened for elementary school children. The book described the program and experiences as perceived by the school personnel, the students, the parents, and college interns. One of the most successful aspects of the program was the compulsory tutoring sessions which were viewed initially as adult tutor to student tutee but later expanded to peer tutoring and cross age tutoring. The open classroom setting is just a miniature model of the Parkway School open education complex.

Gartner, Kohler, and Riessman (1971) concluded that strategy for change is imperative. Learning through teaching works for a great variety of reasons, both cognitive and emotional. For the tutor, it provides feeling of competency and increased self-esteem. The tutee benefits from the increased individualization. In 1971, Pollio and Pollio claimed that children as early as the third grade can use figurative language effectively. Piaget, reviewed in Kamii and DeVries (1973), looked at the biological development of children and claimed fourth graders who are in the concrete operational stage of development are capable of using metaphoric language (highly abstract terms for them) in concrete situations. These findings suggest fourth graders are capable of manipulating language well enough to help a peer. The feasibility of using students to teach students in the individualization of instruction became apparent. Replicating the method of peer tutoring for second language learners is greater in open classrooms where learning centers house curriculum tasks and materials essential to the specific teaching units needed for independent study and work in pairs.

Graubard and Rosenberg (1974), after stating that "an ideal educational system should be able to help every child and conversely, educational systems should not have to reject any child" (p. 1), proceeded to describe classrooms that work for children, classrooms where experiential learning is provided by a facilitative teacher whose role differs much from the traditional teacher. Wittner and Myrick (1974) characterized the role of a facilitating teacher and gave a detailed explanation of the methodology used in open environments. They also offered practical suggestions on how teachers can change their roles from traditional to facilitating in the classroom.

This investigator concurs with the authors who have contributed to the realization that youth has validity (Gartner, Kohler, & Reissman, 1969; Glasser, 1969; Thelen, 1968). The possibilities of equal successes for second language learners in facilitating environments are being explored in this investigation.

Gentry, Jones, Peelle, Phillips, Woodbury, and Woodbury (1972) shared experiences in the Center for Urban Education at the University of Massachusetts at Amherst. They developed new models for urban schools based upon their knowledges of child development in a complex social environment. The overall theme in their book was that children in urban schools could learn in an integrated setting with a teacher in a facilitating role, with flexible scheduling that is individualized, and a new approach to curriculum. "The responsibility of urban school reform is to facilitate the growth of each individual to his fullest potential" (p. 63). Allen (1970) expanded the idea.

> In American education, we have dreamed for at least 150 years of public supported education for all our citizens. For at least three-quarters of a century, we have dreamed of making such education a quality experience. For fifty years or longer, with our sophistication in learning theory and in psychological awareness, we have dreamed of individualizing such education. (p. 63)

The group of writers ended their book with a chapter called "The Hope Factor for Urban Education" where they summarized some of the successes minorities met in urban areas across the country such as Westside Study Center in Pasadena, California, The Human Development Institute (HDI) in Atlanta, Georgia, The Brooklyn Career Opportunities Program and the New Careers Program in New York.

Weinstein and Fantini (1970) reported on their explorations of designing, field testing, reviewing, and analyzing curricula to consider children's affective behaviors. Their evaluation included answers from questionnaires distributed to faculty and students from many schools across the country who had become aware of the human potential movement and meaningful change. Upon careful analysis of the data, the staff concluded "significant contact with pupils is most effectively established and maintained when the content and method of instruction have an affective basis" (p. 10). However, they warn against teachers using random affective techniques with children without adequate training.

In a study conducted by Haynes (1973) on Humanizing Instruction in the Open Classroom, the first years evaluation of the children in a newly organized open environment in grades one through four showed gains only in the affective domain and no gains at the cognitive level. However, the test scores in grades one and three conducted at the end of the second year indicated scores at or above grade level in reading, an indication that cognitive learnings took place.

Betancourt (1975) developed an eclectic approach to instruction in a fourth grade. The children were exposed to four different approaches to learning - the traditional, the semi-open, the open, and

24

learning centers. At the end of the year the class evaluated the four approaches concluding that the choice of approaches was democracy in action. However, the traditional classroom approach created an uneasiness and a change of attitude toward school. The semi-open and learning centers approaches were the most popular.

On March 10, 1974 the Rocky Mountain News of Denver, Colorado, published an article about how children in Honolulu learned to speak English through cooperative cooking experiences. These children, ranging in ages between 18 months to five years of age, communicated spontaneously over the buying, preparation, cooking and eating of simple meals according to the article entitled "Children Learn How to Speak by Cooking."

The Bank Street Follow Through Program attempted to assess the oral and written productive language experiences of children in the Follow Through Program as the experimental group and non-Follow Through as a controlled group. In the article "Language Assessment of EDC Through Children," Weissman (1976) was critical of language instruments were being tested by evaluation teams. The staff administered High/Scope Productive Language Arts tasks designed to measure Reporting and Narrating tasks to 143 third graders. Children were organized into groups of six. For the Reporting tasks, materials or manipulative objects that could be explored and used to create something were given to children to make use of for about 20 minutes. After that time the pupils were to write for 30 minutes about how they made what they made. A pupil checklist form was used and analyzed for any extraneous circumstances that might have interfered with the task. One week later the Narrating task was administered which supplied the children with specific materials to elicit a 30 minute written story beginning with the words "Once upon a time." Again a checklist form followed. The tests were scored by the EDC staff trained in the High/Scope scoring procedures. The results seemed to show Follow Through children wrote more developed narrative stories and had done equally as well on the reporting task as the control group. Much more investigation was recommended and planned.

Educational leaders are recognizing the need to prepare and to continue to train school teachers to meet the new goals for individualization as witnessed by the mandate of state educational agencies for competency based teacher education programs. The intent behind these programs is to build in teacher accountability in the classroom based upon their performance or demonstration of cognitive, affective, and attitudinal competencies. Issues of Educational Leadership have been devoted to disseminating information to supervisors in hopes of bringing an awareness to the realm of effective change. Some of the most recent issues bearing on this topic are:

Educational Leadership: "Curriculum for Economic and Ethnic Diversity" (January 1972); "American Schools vs. Cultural Pluralism" (April 1974, pp. 405-408); "Open Space vs. Self-Contained" (December 1974, pp. 291-295); and "Towards New Goals for Individualization" (January 1975).

Change, a college-wide publication, recognizes the inescapable need for the universities to deal with value problems in improving teacher education. Albert Einstein was cited in Change (September 1974):

It is essential that the student acquire an understanding of and a lively feeling for values. He must acquire a vivid sense of the beautiful and the morally good, otherwise he -

with his specialized knowledge - more closely resembles a
well trained dog than a harmoniously developed person. (p. 29).

This issue continues to support the need for curriculum change in
dealing with materials focusing on life situations in which people
are involved before they accumulate knowledges necessary to ameliorate
life's conditions and shape public policy.

From the many enlightening theories on child development, it is
possible to extract some commonalities in thought in the empirical
findings. The holistic approach to the "total" child acting and reac-
ting within his environment appears throughout the literature. The
child is viewed as a product of his experiences within his native,
cultural environment where language develops sequentially from listening,
speaking, to reading and writing in tune with his biological capabilities
and maturity and his social setting. Reading is viewed as an attitude
and a skill necessary to extend a child's natural curiosity in exploring
his surroundings. Modern linguists and second language teachers are
now attempting to apply these findings in their study of second language
acquisition.

Part III: More Recent Studies in Second Language Acquisition
Influenced by Child Development Theories

Teaching English as a second language (ESL) has been struggling
for recognition and indeed its survival in the United States since
World War II. Looking at the history of ESL movement, it is clearly
evident that this area of concern had adopted an interdisciplinary
approach to education before the concept became as popular as it is
today. Among the specialists having input in the development of ESL
or who have done research in the field were philosophers, anthropologists, linguists, psychologists, speech specialists, sociologists, and
human relations experts. The investigator surveyed, in Chapter II,
these various inputs in the development of English as a second language
in education in the United States from World War II to the present.

Methods on how to teach a second language to reach the goal of
communicative competence have always plagued linguists and second
language teachers. The direct method in the 1940's was an attempt to
replace the old traditional grammar memorization and translation but
"systematically excluded all use of the learner's first language and
attempted to have him learn the foreign language" (Hall, 1960, p. 212).
The phonetic method made "extensive use of highly detailed phonetic
analysis and transcription, and also emphasized intensive oral practice
before beginning to read and write" (p. 212). During the Second World
War the Army Special Training (AST) Program combined language studies
with area studies which was put into effect in many colleges across
the country. The AST Program was an attempt to learn language. This
audio-lingual approach appeared more real but interpretations of reality
involved concepts, values, procedures, rules, facts, and skills.

The Situational Reinforcement method is one of the more recent
methods aimed at "realism" in getting the student to speak using
familiar situations revolving around him and his environment. This
method attempts to incorporate the best of Chomsky's principles of
generating any number of new sentences and Piaget's observation of
children's language that is egocentric and self-directed. It emphasizes
meaning over form and creativity over control. However, this method
is still totally dependent upon the teacher who must contrive situations
where students can achieve the planned, controlled, and desired

26

utterances.

Although the linguists have placed the learning of languages in better perspective yielding more effectiveness in the process, understanding behavior called for not only linguistic skills but psychological, sociological, and cultural factors which are constantly changing. Cultural changes in America resulted from the relaxing of immigration laws and the migration movement from Puerto Rico making it necessary to redefine American society as "a culturally and linguistically, pluralistic society whose members are culturally and linguistically different without any one member or group of members being superior to the other" (Jacobson, 1971, p. 283).

The 1960's brought the first awareness of these sociological factors to the language researchers, namely Hall (1960) and Lado (1964) who were among the first distinguished linguists to recognize and vocalize the need for change in second language teaching. "Phonemes, morphemes, and syntax also change as everything else in the world changes" (Hall, 1960, p. 157). Hall observed the inevitability of language changes pointing up how these changes simultaneously take place with environmental changes. Lado challenged old language laws and theories when he introduced new concepts of individual differences in language learning based upon experiences and inferences from developmental learning research (pp. 38-45). Dynamic language methods began to surface from basic assumptions that language used in the classroom is natural; that structures are supplied and used when needed regardless of difficulty; that language learning is active and is a trial and error process; that reading has a place from the very beginning; and that meaningful materials are motivational.[1]

The 1970's witnessed an important and necessary increase in language studies developing around these new principles of language learning. Ervin-Tripp (1970) reported:

> I think two major changes have taken place in our views of language acquisition in recent years. One is that we now are beginning to see the function of language in the life of the speaker as of far more importance in its acquisition than we had realized, and the other is that the mechanical view that practice makes perfect has given way under the impact of evidence that speechless children can well developed language (a reference to a case study by Lenneberg). (p. 314)

Teachers, in their attempts to use new theories and help children reach the goal of communicative competence, experimented with and employed eclectic methods that were getting results. Rosenbaum (1970) appeared skeptical of eclective approaches when he stated

> effective language instruction presupposes the construction of a learning environment in which is provided properly supervised practice of relevant learning tasks - classrooms are structured around the needs of teachers rather than the needs of students. A most crucial task of language instruction today, therefore, is to devise a new classroom regime capable of satisfying all major language learning environment criteria. (p. 111)

Rosenbaum then described a learning environment conducive to language learning which in essence is the open classroom model.

Jakobovits, cited in <u>TESOL Quarterly</u> (1972, p. 206) regarded the student as the most important contributor to the language learning process, and the teacher the best qualified to decide upon the innovations in instructional procedures and materials that are effective. Brown (1972) expressed interest in the teachers' new role and new approaches "in the classrooms that make maximum appeal to meaningful learning sets within the learners. This appeal should be made on the basis of the total human organism, in the sense that cognitive, affective, and psychomotor processes are all involved" (p. 206). Spolsky (1970) constructed a model for language learning that was consistent with language theories.

Stevick (1975) sought to apply the concept of the holistic approach to the whole learner interacting with materials in a social setting with their peers. According to Richards, strategies of communication are identifiable as an approach when second language learners are communicating with native speakers of the target language (p. 11), or the fact that students communicate best with their peers in very natural settings (Blackburn, 1971; Rivers, 1971; Jakobovitz, 1973; Richards, 1972; Valette, 1973; Milon, 1974). Implications are that maximum peer involvement in classes for pre-pubescent children and minimal teacher involvement would have the best results. The teacher's role is to insure the interaction among language students and native speakers in the class.

Lambert, Just, and Segalowitz (1971) conducted an experiment in Montreal, Canada, with two classes of monolingual English children who received their first years of schooling in French. The kindergarten classes stressed vocabulary development and listening comprehension through art, music, and play, and encouraged spontaneous verbal expressions in French which was the only language used from the first grade on. The results of the experiment indicated

> a high level of skill in both the receptive and productive
> aspects of French, the major language of instruction; a
> generally excellent command of all aspects of English,
> the home language of the children, and a high level of
> skill in non-language subject matter, mathematics taught
> through the foreign language only. (pp. 229-230)

The children even transferred their reading skills from French to English with relative ease. It has been suggested that social differences might have attributed to the Montreal success (Ervin-Tripp, 1971). Because languages verify differences in culture, and since America has been monolingual so long, social judgments are placed on other languages and other dialects. Difficulties for upward mobility in America stem from a degree of social acceptance rather than language according to Hall (1960), Williams (1970), and Richards (1972).

Cultural and linguistic barriers for some groups had become part of the traditional educational system. These groups may have valued cooperation and sharing over competition, uniqueness of the individual over established standards for all, value the socialization of people over personal possession or respected the manual worker equally as well as the professional. In many cases these cultural groups were forced to abandon their language for the prevailing one. Interest in studying existing sociological and social psychological conditions became the job of the sociolinguists, representing a new discipline in an interdisciplinary approach to language learning.

Sociolinguistics is "the study of the characteristics of language varieties, the characteristics of their function and the characteristics of their speakers as these three constantly interact, change and change one another within a speech community" (Fishman, 1972, p. 4). This is an area which is open for additional research on language behavior among subcultural groups. Fishman (1972) sought to integrate the social sciences with all interrelated theories and methods in linguistics relevant to the solution of problems in society. He, in a recent volume, has discussed the social phenomena of dialect and bilingualism and further considered specific aspects of cognitive styles and attitudes toward language. As people speaking a different language immigrate or migrate and become more industrialized, the impact of this massive change alters their values and their language. The language of the job, the church, and the school soon become part of the language at home. Languages that were formerly kept apart begin to influence each other phonetically, lexically, and semantically. Sociolinguists, in their attempt to draw attention to what people actually do with languages in a given speech community, would agree that language learners who want to communicate with a certain group would attempt to learn the language of that group. That means the desire to communicate in social settings is the motivation needed to facilitate learning the desired language with ease.

Within the learning situation in a free atmosphere where roles are often changed, nonlinguistic as well as linguistic behaviors are consistent with children's needs. Fishman sees the variations in verbal interactions occurring in communities as trends toward needed planning and the formation of language policies. Recent political decisions on bilingual education are steps toward seeking solutions to educational language problems.[2]

Reading specialists have been largely unfamiliar with the nature of language and reading in a second language in particular. Research studies which have been mainly ignored in traditional education are now coming under scrutiny by reading specialists. In their search for what produces a competent reader, it became necessary to look at the biological, psychological, sociological, cultural, and linguistic influences on the whole child. Buswell (1922) and Taylor (1965), cited in DeChant (1970), researched the eye movements in children's reading and college adults' reading. They refer to the fixation time (the pause that the eye reaches in order to react to the graphic stimuli) and the movement time (time spent looking ahead) as the nature of the reading process. The length of the pause includes seeing and thinking time. Fixation time for children takes about 90 to 94 percent of the reading time; eye movements account for about 6 to 8 percent of the reading time (pp. 20-21).

Goodman (1970) and Smith (1973) have been two of the most outspoken critics of the explosive, rigid, reading programs and materials that are theoretically contrary to the natural language and reading process. They have endorsed the findings of the scientists in developing reading models for teachers. Goodman maintained that "language is an arbitrary code, a social invention to meet the needs of its users for communication" (pp. 824-825). Goodman (cited in Gunderson, 1970, pp. 107-118) believed reading is a psycholinguistic guessing game that involves interaction between thought and language. He, therefore, believed readers must make mistakes in their guesses of the words that give meaning to any selection. These miscues disrupt meaning temporarily until the reader uses graphic, semantic, and syntactical cues to make sense out of the selection. The better readers make fewer miscues. Goodman (1974) rejects empiricists' studies that judge all curriculum and instruction in terms of believable, measurable changes in behavior. "In reading instruction the goal is not to produce behavior in the form of performance on tests; the goal is comprehension" (p. 827). To Goodman, individualization of instruction is imperative in a culturally pluralistic environment. He advocated different programs for different backgrounds.

Gardner (1975) would agree with Goodman. In her study of reading for native Americans, Gardner favored the language experience approach to reading where children

> produce culturally relevant materials...by labeling
> and dictating sentences and stories. Created works
> coming from children about their culture and environ-
> ment provide the vocabulary for word recognition,
> skills, phonetic analysis, comprehension and study
> skills.

This method has met with success in second language teaching of reading primarily because it stimulated children's natural curiosity to learn more about their own environment. Been (1975), influenced by Chomsky's theory of transformational grammar, accepted the hypothesis that meaning is related to deep structure (true meaning) which does not proceed linearly, because deep structures are abstractions. Logically, then, readers need to perceive whole sentences in order to apprehend deep structure. Recent studies are beginning to stress the importance of true meaning in achieving reading successes.

Smith (1973) claimed that the process of reading involves a reduction of uncertainty about the meaning of a selection. While Goodman used the terminology "Psycholinguistic guessing game," Smith used "hypthosesing" or the process of gambling on a coming letter, word or sentence based upon information expected or concepts developed from verbal or nonverbal experiences. Children, he believed, need to develop large guesses and then small guesses in reducing the intolerance or uncertainty they must face in reading. Implications from these theories are that second language learners like first language learners must have sufficient oral language skills to permit contextual clues, word associations, redundancy, and cognate factors associated with reading to help them become part of the guessing games or hypothesising.

Braun (1971), in his collection of readings delivered at the International Reading Association's Conference, cited authors who are equally concerned about language structure and reading. For instance, Reed found superior scores in reading comprehension of bilingual seventh grade children who had studied syntax and paragraph structures over the scores of those who had not received such instruction. There was substantial evidence from the study to imply a positive relationship between linguistic competence and reading performance. Smith, also cited in Braun (1971), reported on the predictability of a Cloze reading test, where words at regular intervals are missing, that the redundancy and habit formation of the English language is a factor in taking a reading test. He hypothesized that the productive level of syntax structure may determine the best receptive level. Increasingly the productive level of a second language learner is viewed as crucial to his progress in learning to read in English. Elkind (1975), a prominent psychologist and educator, stated that poor readers are poor listeners, thus implying weaknesses at the receptive level of language development be improved through improving the productive level of a student. Yet more emphasis is placed on reading tests and little research has come forth on the productive level of language.

Taylor (1953) was the first to publish a paper on the use of the Cloze test which has since been researched by many others (Oller & Inal, 1971; Potter, 1968; Rankin, 1965; Weintraub, 1968). All of these authors and researchers were seeking to measure reading for diagnostic, teaching, and achievement purposes. Oller (1973) stated that there was a high correlation between a cloze test and other standardized tests. Haskell (1972) concurred with this principle in his testing research. According to Haskell a score of 53 percent or more indicates a child's independent reading ability or competent level, 44-52 percent instructional level, and below 44 percent a frustration level.

Emphasis on humanism in second language teaching and less on specific methodology has become a pervasive theme at recent TESOL conferences especially at the 1975 one in Los Angeles, California. Human relations principles and practices have been recognized by many as freeing students to express feelings with others. A second language speaker in an integrated setting is led to communicate with his peers, and through his communication experiences come to an awareness of the similarities and differences in languages. Through language usage, he can conceptualize his own rules while imitating native pronunciation of the language in the process. Of those who have been purporting these principles are Bouton and Brown (1975), Milon (1974), Oller (1970), Paulston (1974), Puhl (1975), Rivers (1973), and Taylor (1975).

Another prevailing theme at present TESOL conventions is second language acquisition stated as interlanguage where a student hypothesizes from what he knows of the second language rather than what he already knows of the first language. These recent studies point out less dependence upon contrastive analysis of languages and more upon observations and error analysis. In fact, errors in second language usage are an acceptable and desirable necessity to reach the goal of communicative competence (Dulay & Burt, 1974; Ervin-Trip, 1974; Kamii & DeVries, 1973). Linguistic competence for second language learners viewed by these authors, follows communicative competence, a universally accepted theory for first language learners.

Apparently what is also universal is that cultural or social variations reflect individual differences in the application of languages. Speakers use lexical and structural features in profoundly different ways in their conception of the world of reality. This fact points up the uniqueness of each language which impedes literal translations in language systems. The concepts of universal strategies in learning a language are of prime importance to those involved in second language learning and teaching. The findings indicate the need for curriculum developers and language test specialists to give more attention to natural settings for total language development where children are exploring rich meaningful language at school integrating other curriculum areas in the process.

The literature reviewed to date supports the concept that communicative competence precedes linguistic competence which precedes reading competence and this phenomenon is universal. In Lenneberg's (1970) study of biological development of language present in all cultures, sequentially intonation patterns are reproduced first, followed by an awareness of certain articulatory aspects of language in motor development. Children learn through their daily experiences that words bear certain broad relations or specific associations with objects rather than just a name for the object. Furthermore all of these steps in language learning are essential to reading in that language.

Part IV: Future Perspective in Education

Many well known critics of the educational system, Allen, Hentoff, Illich, Toffler, and others (1974) have extrapolated the redundant patterns of traditionalism and the ills of present educational practices in need of change. These authors represent a totality of agreement that education must change concomitantly with society if man is to control his environment, i.e., have more reasonable free choices and sets of options to improve the quality of life everywhere. Education must prepare students to be members of a pluralistic, constantly changing society. Allen (1974), a much publicized educator, stated

> By moving education to a Maslovian psychology of man and
> a new conception of information, we can revise educational
> content to reflect the challenge we will face in the future.
> ...We must revise three of the pervasive educational values:
> our fears of educational change, our myth of educational
> sameness, and our glorification of educational objectivity.
> (p. 10)

He suggested bold new models for making education significant and cross-generational. The models are outlined in detail, but the basic principles underlying the models are:
1. Need to make education cross-generational, diversify and expand our nonformal educational resources, increase the number of sites where education takes place; and add a social service component to education.
2. Need to reorient educational content to a new concept of information and a new psychology of man that will be relevant to tomorrow's world. (p. 5)
Hipple (1974) cited authors who do not necessarily agree that open education is the answer for tomorrow's children, but nevertheless there is a unanimity in thought that social problems of today can only be solved by young people moving to their full potentiality to do the job.
Toffler (1974) edited articles written by a wide range of authors projecting ideas crucial to the open education movement, the need to influence the quality of life in the future and the need to bridge the gap between technological, social, and educational change. Harmon (1974), a researcher for The Futurists, stated those attributes of research important to future studies.
1. Its completeness - within the range of plausibility considering trends and human choices.
2. Its global approach - holistic research methods to accommodate cultural and technological data.
3. Its search for objectivity - employing a diversity of investigators whose individual and cultural biases are different. (p. 126)
Norris (1975) described an open structure school for elementary school pupils in Andover, Massachusetts, called the Bancroft School where 75 to 100 children with a team of three teachers worked in long rooms called "lofts." There were six lofts corresponding to six learning levels where students may progress at their own speed across any one of the levels needed for him to achieve. Full records were kept on each child's individual progress. The Bancroft School model reflected the efforts of a successful collaboration between architectural and educational ideas worthy of duplication if new child development and language development theories are to be implemented. Conventional schools as buildings or institutions are an anachronism

for the purposes and functions of education for the real world.

Bronfenbrenner (1975) made a plea for a reorientation of theory and research in socialization that would be interdisciplinary in nature. His research model included three dimensions:

1. The immediate setting of the child viewed along the dimensions of physical space and materials; people in differing roles and relationships around the child; and the activities and social meaning of the activities in which the child and others are engaged.

2. Social networks and institutions as peer groups, circle of friends, and neighborhoods.

3. Idealogical system which both explicitly and implicitly endows motivational meaning to social networks, institutions, roles, activities, and their interrelationships. (pp. 447-448)

A humanistic thought that grew out of the interdependence of the humanistic and the futuristic movements is, "The physical, intellectual, emotional, and ethical integration of the individual into a complete man is a broad definition of the fundamental aim for education" (Faure et al., 1972, p. 156).

The role of the linguists in the futuristic movement will be to help educators understand the internalization of grammar of a speaking, listening individual and evaluate affective content of linguistic structures leading to expression in everyday speech. Increased research in nonverbal visual communication will continue as the information theory becomes more and more inevitable. The information theory, a contribution by the anthropologists, "is drawing educators' attention more and more to the anatomy of communication" (Faure et al., 1972, p. 114). This latter theory focuses on the construction of teaching sequences and daily communication between teacher and pupil, whatever the means of transmission involved which may include use of teaching manuals for learning, educational radio and television, audio-visual teaching machines, and language laboratories. Cybernetics is a relatively new terminology in education that deals with the self-regulating individual viewed in micro systems and institutions confronting individual differences or readily identifiable in macro systems (Faure et al., 1972).

Languages will become increasingly more important in a pluralistic society as expressed by Stauffer (1971). Language can help recall the past, represent the present, and anticipate the future. Through the reading process conceptual intelligence can and does become socialized to permit the sharing of whole cultures. LeFevre (1970) reported the need for an interdisciplinary approach to the study of language so that language will become functional in terms of human concerns and activities. As bilingual and cross-cultural programs continue to expand on the educational front, more and more individuals will become bilingual or multilingual and thus more multicultural. Cultural anthropologists will continue to help educators formulate interdisciplinary educational methods on which to base school programs for heterogeneous, cultural, pluralistic societies expected in the future. Futurists (already identified as transdisciplinary) will continue to help man understand himself and his purpose in life.

It is possible to summarize much of the related literature with the observation that the open education concept has provided the impetus for the growth of ideas in recent years about the need to facilitate educational environments in the field of acquisition of a language, and particularly English as a second language.

Specialists in the field of language teaching methodology agree that an open classroom climate provides a factor of crucial importance

in language learning. Proponents of the concept have pointed specifically to spoken language techniques and the integrating of language
learning with the needs of society and the daily life of students when
stimulated by interest aroused in an open classroom climate (Friedl,
1944). For successful growth of ESL see TESOL bulletins (bibliography).
There is inherent in the history of research in child development
potential for developing an open classroom climate in ESL representing
a mode of language learning that could hold promise for more effective
teaching practices.

When open classroom and TESOL are viewed as interdependent with
the changes in the humanistic and futuristic movements in our pluralistic society, there will be no mistaking the fact that an open classroom
climate can provide language learning facilitation in a manner that is
quite acceptable to the individual student.

FOOTNOTES

1 Drawn from ideas of M. Frank at Institute of Modern Languages
  held in New York by Modern Language Associates, September 28, 1974.

2 The Federal Bilingual Education Act (1968); the Massachusetts
  Transitional Bilingual Education Act (1971); Bilingual Education
  as a result of the Supreme Court's decision in Lou vs. Nichols, San
  Francisco, California, Aspira vs. Board of Education, New York
  (1974).

CHAPTER III

THE SUBJECTS, THE MATERIALS, AND THE PROCEDURES

Introduction

The purpose of this chapter was
1. to describe the subjects involved in the study, the socio-cultural and socioeconomic characteristics of the group, and information about their instruction date;
2. to describe the method used in the selection of the subjects;
3. to describe the procedures employed in preparing, distributing, collecting, analyzing, and reporting on the various instruments used in the study;
4. to describe the statistical procedures employed.

The Subjects

In October 1974 the New York City Board of Education conducted the yearly ethnic breakdown of the public schools. The schools in this study are shown in Table 1. Schools A, B, C, and D had the experimental classrooms; A and E had the control groups.

The French speaking children from Haiti had been counted with the Black population. Therefore, there is no category indicating the percentage of Haitians in the schools.

The subjects in this study represented a small sampling of the 102,440 New York City children having moderate language difficulties in learning the English language as indicated by the special study

Table 1

New York City Board of Education Ethnic Breakdown for
Schools in the Study (1974)

School	Total Population	Chinese Percent	Spanish Speaking Percent	Black Percent	Other Percent
A	1794	2.00	44.00	43.00	11.00
B	950	.63	62.32	26.00	11.05
C	1079	3.52	34.75	30.05	31.68
D	968	1.65	41.84	31.00	25.51
E	1140	.86	20.00	69.14	10.00

in 1973 (New York City, Board of Education). Forty children from five schools and eight classes met the criteria set fourth for the study, i.e., fourth graders rated "C or D" on the New York City Language

Rating Scale working in integrated classrooms. The average age was 9-1/2 years out of a range of 9 to 11 years. Of the 40 children, 20 were located in traditional classrooms which became the control group. Of the 20, 12 were boys and 8 were girls. Seven Haitian children from French speaking backgrounds, one from Santo Domingo, and 12 from Puerto Rico with Spanish speaking backgrounds became part of the study. From schools A and E (see Table 1) in one school district, 14 children were rated "C" and six rated "D" coming from three different classrooms. Four of the children were born in the United States; six were in New York two years or less; and 10 were in New York 2-1/2 to 5 years.

Twenty children from five open classrooms within four schools, A, B, C, and D (see Table 1) spanning two school districts became the experimental group. Of the 20, 12 were girls and 8 were boys. Of this group, six were from Haiti, one from Hong Kong with Chinese speaking background, one from Thailand with a Thai speaking background, 12 Spanish speakers of which 9 were from Puerto Rico, 2 from Santo Domingo, and 1 from Cuba. These children from five open classrooms were frequently observed to determine what verbal and nonverbal communicative performances in the classroom environment contributed to the achievement of communicative competence and linguistic competence. Of this group, 14 were rated "C" and six were rated "D". Eight of the 20 children were born in the United States. Five were in New York two years or less, and seven lived in New York 2-1/2 to 5 years.

The schools from which the students were selected were located in integrated areas having a large percentage of second language learners of Spanish origin, French origin, and Chinese origin, listed in order of population dominance. The class sizes ranged from 28 to 32 children per class. Two of the schools housing the experimental classes in one district were situated in areas in transition from middle to low socioeconomic level. Many middle class families living in the area had chosen private schools while some had become interested in the open classroom with its integrated setting. Those who had chosen to continue their children in the public schools gave much support to the new concept within the school. The other two schools were more socioeconomically disadvantaged, i.e., more of the children were from economically deprived homes.

Traditionally, if the language learner, not involved in a bilingual program, received any language instruction, it was done in several ways. The classroom teacher gave him English language instruction some part of the school day; the paraprofessional helped him in following lessons conducted in the classroom; the trained teacher of English as a second language (TESL) removed him from the regular class for lessons emphasizing various aspects of the English language. Because there were fewer opportunities for classroom interaction in the regular classroom, the child was completely dependent upon the classroom teacher for English practice exercises. In the early grades frequent physical mobility facilitated the use of language, but as these creative approaches to language development gave way to more abstract learning and less physical mobility, it was more difficult for the second language learner to develop the cognitive skills in language necessary to succeed in the middle grades. For this reason fourth grade children representing the middle grades were selected.

The Materials

The materials used to conduct this study consisted of a language rating scale designed to rate pupils' ability to speak in English (see Appendix A), a Cloze reading test (see Appendix B), a teacher questionnaire (see Appendix C), a screening and placement form (see Appendix D), and a parent interview form (see Appendix E).

The New York City Language Rating Scale had been used by the Board of Education since 1957 to determine the English speaking proficiency of a second language learner mainly for placement purposes. Classroom teachers administered and rated the children based upon their judgment of the children's structural patterns, vocabulary, intonation patterns, pronunciation, and comprehension demonstrated in conversations with the children. As the TESL program grew in the schools, the TESL teacher, trained in ESL methods and techniques, was responsible for rating the children. A criterion-reference Rating Scale of Pupil's Ability to Speak English has been devised recently as a result of the Aspira Case (1974) to help teachers better determine the level of each child under linguistically set categories for determining oral proficiency. The aim here was to reduce the amount of subjectivity that was formally infused in a child's language rating. The new form came out after this study had begun and was, therefore, not used for the pretest or posttest (see Appendix F).

The process of taking a piece of reading material and deciding if it is appropriate for the group is the first step in planning for a Cloze reading test. The next step is to delete every "x" word for students to complete. In this study every sixth word was deleted from a story having a total of 50 blanks. The passage was selected from a Holt, Rinehart and Winston textbook entitled A Time for Friends, because the words and content were comparable to the children's real experiences within the environment or in other words the selection reflected an integral part of the home, school, and community. The passage also reflected a culture free learning milieu through which a child can communicate his real shared experiences and concerns through reading, one facet of communication in language. It is important to note here that preparation of tests in language learning is difficult to validate because of the theoretical question of the nature of language acquisition. Also in many situations testing is closely related to teaching. When a child is asked to demonstrate his abilities in language acquisition, he is being tested. However, the Cloze reading method of assessing reading comprehension has been tested often for its reliability with second language learning. It determines the readability and comprehension of the student, because it tests the whole process of reading (creativity, intelligence, concept development, and thinking); it considers use of words (some words deleted may be functional or content); and it permits guessing because of the redundancy of the English language.

Scoring for a Cloze reading test can be done in either of three ways. Synonym scoring means acceptability of the use of a synonym to fill in the blank. Verbatim scoring means the exact words must be used, and the third scoring means acceptability of any appropriate word that would fit into the passage. The latter scoring method was used in this study mainly, because it was the easiest for students who were unfamiliar with this type of test. Two points for each of the 50 blanks that fit the passage determined the score. Fifty-three percent or more indicated a competent reading level, 44 to 52 percent equalled the instructional level of reading, and below 44 percent indicated a frustration level. Spelling errors were not counted wrong.

The teacher questionnaire (see Appendix C) was an adaptation of a questionnaire used by Bank Street College in their Follow Through Program during 1960 and 1970. It was divided into three main categories. The first section consisting of 15 items sought information to determine the educational background of the teacher, the program, and the children in the class. The second section consisting of seven items sought to determine what materials were available or on order for effective instruction in the classroom. The third section consisting of six items sought information about the parent-teacher relationships within the school, the classroom, and the program in the particular classroom. Substituting English as a Second Language as a field of interest in place of Follow Through Program constituted the major change in the original Bank Street College questionnaire. This change came primarily in the first section seeking information about teaching experiences and training for such specialized classes.

The purpose behind the screening and placement form devised at the time the Puerto Rican Study was active (1953-57) was to acquire information about each child's birth place, age, sex, language spoken at home, previous schooling somewhere else, present school placement, and attendance patterns. The form had 29 items to be answered (see Appendix D). Upon presentation of all the instruments to be used to the central Board of Education, Research Division, who considered the original form too personal and quite controversial, only those items relevant to this study were maintained. The information was supplied by the classroom teacher or the pupil when interviewed by the investigator. Official pupil records were not available in some cases depending on the school's policy. However, the pupils or their parents were capable of supplying the needed information.

The parent interview form (see Appendix E) contained 10 main items with subdivisions. This form was used by Bank Street College's Follow Through Program in 1970 to bring some insight into how parents perceive the child's relationship to the school and the home. Since understanding the whole child is a pervasive task in the open education concept, this instrument was designed to help bridge the gap between two frames of reference, the teacher's and the parents', to the child's learning interests and abilities. Item no. 10 was deleted from the original form since parents seemed to have difficulties understanding how to rank school related objectives in order of importance to them.

Parent interview forms were translated into French and Spanish for those parents who had not mastered the English language well enough to read in that language. The forms were given to all of the children in the experimental group to take home with a covering letter asking parent cooperation in conducting the study. Fifty-five percent of the parents responded to the questionnaire.

Procedures

The major procedures employed in this study included the planning of the proposal, the selection of the samples, the gathering and developing of the instruments used, the collection of the data, the analysis, synthesis, and reporting of the data, and finally the conclusions and recommendations based upon the findings.

Step I - Planning

The fact that English speaking children were benefitting from their experiences in a child centered room led to examining ways in which second language learners could also benefit from this arrangement. Prior experiences with open education and concern about the "C and D" language learners' inability to read adequately enough to keep up with their peers in the middle grades prompted the development of the proposal for this dissertation. Interest was further stimulated upon visiting an open classroom containing second language learners and observing children interacting with each other and to their environment while concurrently sharing cultural differences including learning another language. Current literature indicated a trend toward the socialization process in communication and toward the holistic view of a child's learning process. With all of these broad ideas about the possibility of children acquiring a second language more effectively in an open classroom environment and thus influence change in education, the study was approved by the administration at Heed University, the Board of Education of New York City (Research Division), two local school board superintendents, members of a local school board, principals, and teachers of schools and finally parents.

Step II - Selection of the Samples

Severe limitations were placed on the investigator when trying to find second language learners rated "C and D" in open classrooms at the fourth grade level based upon the schools' ethnic breakdown and placement policies. Many classrooms were investigated but few met the criteria set for this study. As a result the experimental sampling of 20 students involved five classrooms located in four schools in two districts in New York City. The sampling from traditional classrooms was relatively easy to select. Although the majority of the second language learners was located in mostly homogeneous, regular classrooms, the 20 children selected as the control group came from heterogeneous classrooms consisting of native English speakers as well as second language learners. All of the children in the control group were removed from their regular classes by the TESL teacher some part of the school day for special English instruction.

Step III - Gathering and Development of Instruments Used

A survey of literature and testing instruments indicated that certain information was necessary to provide as authentic a study as possible. Revisions were made of some of the instruments as indicated below.

The New York City Language Rating Scale had already been used by the classroom teacher or the TESL to assess the second language learners' proficiency in speaking English. This scale had been used in the schools from the time the Puerto Rican Study (1953-57) implemented its program in 1957. At the end of the school year, the teachers used the same scale to rate the children.

A reading selection, from a series of stories which were considered of high interest to English speaking children, was chosen. The story revealed the possibilities of its use for second language learners of the same age and grade as their English speaking partners who first took the test. The reading test was administered by the investigator. The children were taken from their classrooms to a designated area. They were told that they were part of a special study and would not be graded on this test by or for the teacher. A variety of cookies was supplied before and after the test to put the children in a relaxed atmosphere. Because of the newness of this type of test, the difficulty of the passage and the length of the test, suggestions were made to skip those blanks that were not known and then return to them later. Sample exercises explaining the uniqueness of the test were provided for all present. The children were given sufficient time to complete the test. During the period of time the children were working, it was observed that less frustration was exhibited by the children from the open classroom and a great deal of determination to fill all blanks. On the other hand most of the children from the traditional classrooms had to be constantly encouraged, because they were more apt to give up.

Step IV - Collection of Data

Initial visits to the five schools and eight classrooms were to meet the children who had become part of this study; to distribute letters to their parents outlining the purpose of the study, the procedures, and the responsibilities of outcomes that would be beneficial to their children specifically and to second language learners in New York City; and to finally administer the Cloze reading pretest. Other visits throughout the year focused on the immediate open classrooms and the second language learners therein who had become the experimental group. Long periods of observations, record keeping, and classroom involvement pursued. Occasionally the tape cassette was used to record conversations between peers or between teacher and student in various learning centers. Later in the study written observations replaced the tape cassette, because the recording instrument too often tended to distract attention from the other children's tasks at hand.

Frequent personal observations were made of the children's involvement in the open classroom during the school year, assessing such intrinsic child related variables as: need to learn English, interest in learning it, ability to consistently grow in the new language, mutual trust and mutual respect in the interaction process in an open classroom. Personal notes were taken describing the room arrangement, materials available, use of materials, conversations among children, talks with teachers, children and parents. Often children, seeing another adult in the classroom, expressed a desire for the person to hear an oral reading selection or to talk about class events, projects, or trips.

The final visits to the open classrooms consisted of recording the language ratings, administering the Cloze reading posttests, and collecting parent and teacher interview forms. The posttest procedure was followed up in the traditional classes with children who comprised the control group. In administering the posttests, fewer anxieties were exhibited partially because the test was not new, the investigator was not new, and the cookies that were anticipated were available. School visits did not terminate until all 40 children in the study had been retested.

Step V - Analysis, Synthesis and Reporting of Data

An analysis was made of all the data collected to determine whether there were any significant differences or relationships between the open classroom with respect to second language acquisition. The information was recorded, synthesized and later reported in Chapter IV of this dissertation.

The statistical methodology used to test for significant differences in achievement in the open class and the traditional class was the (1) t test for independence, (2) correlated t test and (3) the analysis of covariance.

The t test for independence was used to determine if there was a significant difference in the end of the year scores (posttest on the Cloze Reading Test) between the open classroom pupils and the traditional classroom pupils. Assuming a significant difference had occurred, it was necessary to know how much of the increased achievement could be associated with the treatment (open versus traditional). The measure used to determine this strength of association is called Hays Estimate (Hays, 1963, pp. 327-328).

The correlated t test was used to determine significant differences in achievement from pretest to posttest for the two different treatments (open/traditional) separately.

Finally the analysis of covariance f test was used to determine significant differences in achievement between the open class pupils and the traditional class pupils. Researchers want to insure that differences between treatments are genuinely within the limits of error surrounding the treatment. Sometimes the pupils as a group in a given treatment bias the results because of an uncontrollable causal circumstance. The situation arises frequently when Title I treatments are applied to entire classrooms which contain whole classes with different starting levels of achievement. When the samples of disadvantaged learners cannot be controlled through random assignment, matching by pairs, etc., a statistical "control" is introduced "to adjust" the two populations so they could be compared for growth. In other words, the initial level (pretest) before a treatment for a class (open/traditional) may be different, so that an adjustment would have to be made to offset differences in achievement that are attributable to the differences at the initial level. Thus, the analysis of covariance was used to remove the bias that favors one class over another at the outset of a treatment.

Step VI - Concluding the Study

This investigation used a multifaceted approach involving extensive theoretical and critical discussions of a host of neuropsychological, cognitive, social, cultural, and affective considerations viewed as central to a comprehensive model of an idealized design of a language learning environment. The critical discussions found in Chapter II, Review of the Related Literature, served as the starting point for the experimental part of the study. The last stages of this research summarized the procedures, drew conclusions, and made recommendations based upon the data collected throughout the school year.

CHAPTER IV

FINDINGS

Introduction

The purpose of this chapter was to analyze the data of the study
with respect to the problems posed in Chapter I; to report the empirical and scientific findings; and to discuss supportive statements
leading to the evaluative effectiveness of the study. The problems
posed in Chapter I are:

1. In what way does language instruction for the second language
learners in open classrooms differ from the formal aural-oral language
instruction given in traditional classrooms?

2. What is the relationship between the open classroom organizational plan and the achievement of communicative competence and
linguistic competence?

3. In what way did second language learners in the fourth grade
grow cognitively in the open classroom?

4. What were the differences between the two groups on the pretests and posttests of the language rating scale and the Cloze reading
test?

Questions to Be Answered

Question 1

In what way does language instruction for second language learners
in open classrooms differ from the formal aural-oral language instruction given in traditional classrooms?

One recognizable difference between language usage in the open
classrooms and the traditional classroom was the general awareness of
the importance of language in a social environment that was less
threatening to students. In this free atmosphere there was a constant
hum of voices as students used language to communicate to one another
or to their teachers. Language lessons were not taught to language
learners separately and apart from the rest of the group. Second
language learners, in the process of acquiring a second language, had
human and environmental input contributing to their oral productive
level and to their motivation to read for further knowledge. Other
recognizable differences could be discussed best by examining the
four interrelated components in an open classroom: (1) the teachers,
(2) the children, (3) the curriculum and (4) the parents.

The teachers. The information supplied by the teachers' questionnaire indicated that all of the teachers in the experimental group had
over three years experience in a classroom, had been trained in open
education philosophy, and had taught minority children. Not one of
the teachers had any training in English as a second language. All of
the teachers enjoyed working in an atmosphere where the children were
ethnically integrated and believed the open classroom was "ideal" for
using language on a social level. One teacher commented on the amount

of time required to keep records and measure pupil progress. One
teacher preferred a lower adult-pupil ratio in the classroom. One was
critical of the rigid school schedules in New York City public schools
which negate some of the basic philosophies of an open environment.
All of the experimental teachers recommended continuing the program
with some modifications based upon on-going evaluations. There was
an unanimity of opinions that the program needed more materials to
continue satisfying children's interests in manipulating objects.

According to the teachers, parents, who had been introduced to
the open classroom concept, made the choice to place their children
in open classrooms, and therefore were interested in becoming involved
in some way. Teachers conducted workshops for parents to help them
guide their children through the parents' own awareness of the purposes
and goals of the program.

The teachers in the open classroom planned the learning experiences
for all of the children including the language learners. There was no
fragmentation of learning for second language learners or isolation
from the regular classroom for special language lessons. The teachers
were not "modeling" language patterns for students to repeat in large
groups or small groups. Instead teachers shifted roles at will throughout the day from a teacher to a mother, a nurse, a psychologist, a
model, a counselor, or a facilitator in dealing with individual children
and their on-the-spot needs.

Discussions which usually are directed and structured by the
traditional classroom teachers were often initiated by the children
in the open classroom. Because the teachers knew each child's strengths
and weaknesses, they did not judge them on their verbal ability alone
but rather on their own contributions as they actively and curiously
moved about exploring their immediate environment. The teachers
focused on the whole child as an individual learner as well as a
member of the group. The individualization of the learning process
permitted the teachers to focus on educational needs of children for
which provisions were made for children to develop cognitive competencies so closely related to linguistic competencies.

In the open classrooms studied, the teachers were diligently
preparing materials for use, checking assignments, offering suggestions,
encouraging better performances, monitoring classroom schedules and
performing other necessary tasks for maximum effectiveness or efficiency.
Very often team teaching and peer tutoring methods were used to facilitate learning as lessons spilled out into the corridors. The second
language learners became tutees during peer tutoring sessions, but
occasionally roles changed and the "C" rated child would be seen tutoring another child. Teachers met regularly with each other to discuss
individual children's needs, record keeping, testing instruments,
ordering and sharing of materials, or to exchange ideas. It was quite
evident that continuous training of teachers and supportive services
contributed to well organized open classrooms described in this
dissertation.

The children. It was not always easy to identify the second
language learners in the open classroom. Instead of being isolated,
the students were actively involved in a setting that provided constant
human interaction. Self-motivation moved children to exchange bits of
information needed to perform certain tasks. There were no limits to
the opportunities to grow cognitively in the various learning centers.
The classrooms provided a variety of materials and wholesome emotional
environment where children had positive images of themselves and a

sense of worth. Emotions were not suppressed in any way. Children expressed happiness, love, anger, fear, joy, and anxieties as they would at home. In many cases these emotions were quickly dealt with at the moment of need. Children had the freedom to agree or disagree, to have instant gratification or postpone "knowing" until such time as the need was felt. Children felt free to read aloud to each other or on a one-to-one basis with an adult, because there was a sense of achievement in an atmosphere of cooperation. In fact a great deal of enthusiasm developed from the freedom of expression, freedom of choice and movement which inspired reading for further information coming from a variety of sources.

The curriculum. The curriculum in the open classroom was designed around learning centers which were set up with a diversity of commercial materials, children-made materials and teacher-made materials. All of these materials were out and in constant use. Language became not only a tool for communication but also the tool for acquiring knowledge amidst human interaction. The classroom reflected the integrated approach to learning which was more natural to life and living than in the traditional classroom where the curriculum was prescribed; where materials were locked in closets restricting their use; where children were expected to speak only when called upon; and where whole sets of materials were ordered, one for each child.

Learning in the open environment was not confined to the classroom only. It spilled out into the corridors, neighboring classrooms, parks, museums and a variety of other places of interest. Within this environment of human interaction, messages were transmitted verbally and nonverbally. Language in all of its forms was the necessary vehicle to help a child acquire knowledge. A word supplied on the spot or a phoneme to clarify the meaning of a word or sentence structure being imitated were witnessed while children related to materials and to their peers.

The five open classrooms exhibited a range of interesting activities in which children were freely engaged. These classrooms had on-going projects into which children made many contributions. The projects became conversation pieces as all children expressed joy over their own personal contributions, but especially the second language learner who had an opportunity to use language in a variety of forms to express his contributions or describe the project to his peers, teachers and visitors. The following cooperative tasks initiated by the children were on display in the classrooms visited.
1. Taino Indian Village
2. An African Village
3. History of the Airplane
4. Prehistoric Animals
5. Parts of the Human Body
6. Study of Bones
7. Creative Kites

Work that was exhibited in each of the classroom projects was done in the various learning centers which had similar activities going on within different room arrangements. Children were scheduled to participate in each activity planned jointly by them and the teacher. The learning centers were easily identifiable by the type of activities and the materials available at all levels of interest and all levels of ability. Free heterogeneous grouping in the classrooms and in the learning centers motivated the successes children were experiencing and were adjusting to readily.

One classroom had blocks for building, two had typewriters, one a T.V. set and one a puppet stage. In one class the children contructed a miniature store with a counter and a mathematics computer to transact business. This class ran a series of fund raising activities such as cake, candy and punch sales, to purchase more materials for class use. Musical instruments were often used as children played and sang a variety of ethnic songs especially during special days or holidays. Most of the noisier activities such as wood working, poster painting, clay molding, cardboard carpentry and drama activities, took place in the corridors.

The trained Teacher of English as a Second Language knew the importance of manipulative materials, human dialogues, and freedom of movement to the language learner. But, the responsibility of servicing the large number of language learners in a school meant scheduling children for special times during the day or during the week. During these times the children were isolated from their classmates, exposed to prescribed language lessons for repetitive drills in a contrived setting. The children rated "C" were often removed from the TESL to make room for a more recent arrival. Those "C" children in traditional classrooms were placed in the lowest exponent on the grade because of their poor reading performance. The children rated "C" in the open classrooms described above were in heterogeneous groupings using language skills, encoding and decoding in a social learning atmosphere without the fear of failure under highly competitive conditions found in most traditional classrooms. The emphasis was reaching educational needs and goals necessary to adapt to the world of reality with competence and self-confidence.

The parents. On an interview form, parents were asked to select one of five categories (never, very rarely, sometimes, very often, always) which best described their particular child. The responses have been totaled and the percentages recorded on the parent interview form (see Appendix E). However, the majority of the parents indicated that the children very often talked about other children and about things they made in school; sometimes started discussions about school, about the teacher, about special events and sometimes took home things made at school; never wanted to stay home from school and never had to be coaxed in order to get ready for school. Indications were that children were peer conscious and were enjoying going to school to meet their friends.

Of the 15 school related activities children like to do at home without being asked, block building, cooking or telephoning classmates to discuss school work apparently were rarely done in these second language learners' homes. Cultural reasons and/or economic conditions probably bore some relationship to why these activities were not engaged in at home.

Question 2

What is the relationship between organizational plan of the open classroom and the achievement of communicative competence and linguistic competence?

The freedom of movement, expression, choice and speech witnessed in an open classroom provided the necessary classroom interaction for the second language learners to communicate with their peers in their own language or in the second language. Verbal fluency and nonverbal communication played a major role in observing children in this study.

Language usage and syntactical structures, simple or difficult, were used in the course of asking questions, answering questions, changing tenses, giving commands, moving from singular to plural, and changing from first person to third person. There was evidence of the use of figurative expressions and a more advanced use of language.

The second language learners had the freedom to make errors wherein some were corrected on the spot. Other errors went unnoticed unless they hindered communication. In the course of many conversations, the correct phoneme, morpheme or sentence structure were used by the teacher or an English speaking peer. The language learner took the opportunity to imitate the corrected form very much as how the first language is heard and imitated in middle income families where mothers build upon or correct a child's language. When children were groping for the right word or expression, these aspects of language were supplied immediately. Observations were made of this linguistic performance in the sharing of knowledge and skills in the various learning centers. In the socialization process prevalent in the centers, second language learners were becoming competent in their ability to communicate specific directions, explain what tasks they had accomplished, describe on-going projects, discuss trips to outside places, role play, exchange ideas in general and use their second language for their own purposes rather than listening to or repeating after a "model." No emphasis was placed upon speaking in whole sentences. Instead, association in these fourth grades brought on assimilation from the sociolinguistic point of view. Within this communication, children were exposed to phonological and lexical variations in the English language which created no problem with them. Dialectical differences were acceptable and used in conversations.

Skill lessons in the form of workbook exercises, oral reports, task cards, reading and writing exercises in all of the curriculum areas were provided for the improvement of various learning skills. The tasks were assigned based upon individual needs. Language learners were not given any special attention. Instead they were improving needed linguistic skills along with their native English speaking peers. It was within these working sessions that peer tutoring took place. The paired lessons drew attention to syntactic structures which generally posed problems in the encoding and decoding processes of learning a new language. In fact these lessons pointed up the needs of the native English speaking child to better his own linguistic skills if he was going to be an effective tutor. Both groups looked forward to these tutoring sessions. The tutors were experiencing teaching as an occupation or profession. Some of the tutors expressed a desire to become teachers having been encouraged by successful sessions with their partners. Some did not mind helping a friend but were convinced that teaching would not be their career goal. The tutees were enjoying the special attention.

What was significant during the observation period was the language progress the children were making. To a number of persons who visited frequently or occasionally, amazement was uttered at the rapid progress children had made during the term. Some children changed behavior from shyness to active, aggressive learners.

Question 3

What are the differences in achievement between the two groups from the pretests to the posttests of the New York City Language Rating Scale and the Cloze reading test?

The achievement test results on the Cloze Reading Test were analyzed using (1) the t test for independent samples with a follow-up called Hays estimate, (2) the t test for correlated means, and (3) the analysis of covariance F test. (See Table 2)

Table 2

Analysis of the Posttest Scores for the Open Classroom
Versus the Traditional Classroom Using the t Test
for Independence (Cloze Reading Test)

Treatment	Size of Sample	Posttest Mean	Standard Deviation	t Value	Level of Significance
Open Classroom	20	72.2	14.53		
				4.75	p $<$ .01
Traditional Classroom	20	40.3	26.39		

$w^2 = .35$

The scores ranged from 36 to 94 on the posttest for the open classroom pupils and 2 to 74 for the pupils in the traditional classrooms. The posttest mean was 72.2 with a standard deviation of 14.53, while the posttest mean for the traditional classroom was 40.3 and the standard deviation of 26.39. The difference in the mean grades was 31.9 which when transformed to a t statistic was t = 4.75. This t value (t = 4.75) was significant at the .01 level, which indicated that the open classroom pupils achieved significantly higher than the traditional classroom pupils; Hays estimate (w^2) was also determined to see how much of this increased achievement could be associated with the open classroom environment. This estimate yielded a value of .35 which means that the open classroom treatment appeared to account for about 35 percent of the obtained score. Statistically the value of .35 was significant. (See Table 3)

Table 3

Analysis of the Pre/Post Scores for the Open Classroom and the
Traditional Classroom Using a Correlated t Ratio
(Cloze Reading Test)

Treatment	Size of Sample	Pretest Mean	Posttest Mean	Difference Post-Pre	t Value	Level of Significance
Open Classroom	20	59.3	72.2	12.9	3.11	p $<$ .01
Traditional Classroom	20	34.6	40.3	5.7	1.92	Not significant

Open classroom treatment. The scores ranged from 18 to 92 in the open classroom on the pretest. The pretest mean for the open classroom pupils was 59.3 and the posttest mean was 72.2, an increase in achievement of 12.9 points. The difference (12.9) in the mean grades was converted to a correlated t statistic ($t = 3.11$). This t value of 3.11 was significant at the .01 level, which indicated that a significant increase in achievement had occurred from pre- to posttesting.

Traditional classroom treatment. Scores ranged from 0 to 78 on the pretest for traditional classroom pupils. The pretest mean was 34.6 and the posttest mean was 40.3, an increase in achievement of 5.7 points. The difference (5.7) in the mean grades was converted to a correlated t statistic ($t = 1.92$). This t value of 1.92 was not significant, which indicates that even though there was some increase in the grades of the pupils from pre- to posttesting, the increase was not statistically significant.

The analysis of covariance (Anacova) F test was used to determine whether there was any significant difference in achievement between the open classroom and the traditional classroom, while controlling for any initial differences (pretest results) in the two groups.

By taking into account any initial differences in achievement (pretest scores), it became necessary to adjust the posttest results for the two treatments (see Table 4). The F value for the Anacova was calculated to be 11.18, which is statistically significant at the .01 level. Thus this analysis implied that the achievement for the open classroom pupils was significantly higher than the achievement for the traditional classroom pupils, based on the results of the Cloze Reading test instrument.

Table 4

Analysis of the Posttest Scores for the Open Classroom
Versus the Traditional Classroom Using the
Analysis of Covariance F Test Design[a]
(Cloze Reading Test)

Source of Variance	Sum of Squares	Adjusted Degrees of Freedom	Mean Square	F Value	Level of Significance
Between groups	6,101	1	1,857		
				11.18	p $\angle$ .01
Within groups	24,326	37	166		

Treatment	Adjusted Posttest Means
Open Classroom	63.8
Traditional Classroom	48.7

[a]The initial differences (pretest scores) were used as the covariate measure.

48

The findings resulting from the language rating scale indicated significant gains made by the experimental group as compared to the control group (see Figure 1). In the open classroom environment six children moved from "D" rating to "C"; the other 14 children moved out of the category designated for language learners (see Appendix A). The teachers rated one "A", three "B+" and 10 "B." (See Figure 3). In the traditional classroom one child remained "D" in the posttest out of the six; five moved to "C"; four from "C" to "C+"; and seven to "B" (see Figure 2). According to the findings seven children from the control group were no longer considered language learners by their classroom teachers. The teachers of both groups voluntarily placed a plus (+) after a letter grade, because they felt children did not measure up to the top grade but were more than the lower one.

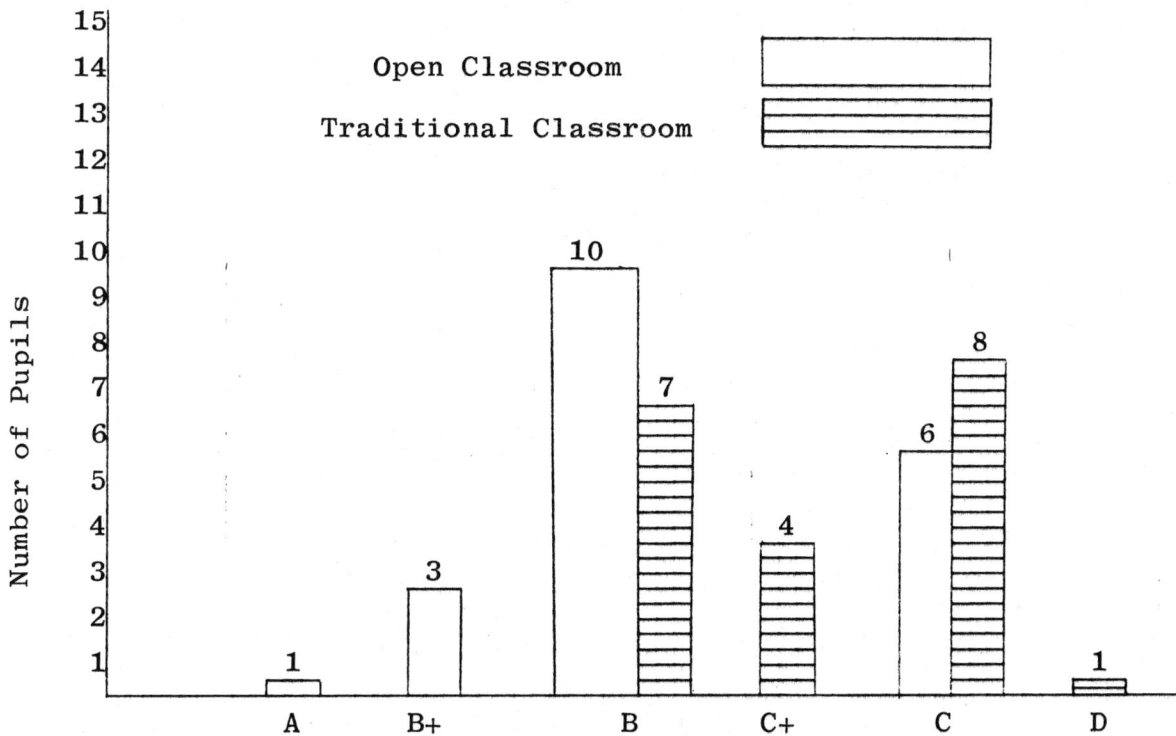

Figure 1. A histogram depicting the posttest results for the open classroom versus the traditional classroom: Oral Language Rating Scale (n = 20).

Rating Scale

15
14
13
12
11
10
9
8
7
6
5
4
3
2
1

Number of Pupils

7

4

14

8

6

1

A   B+   B   C+   C   D

Rating Scale

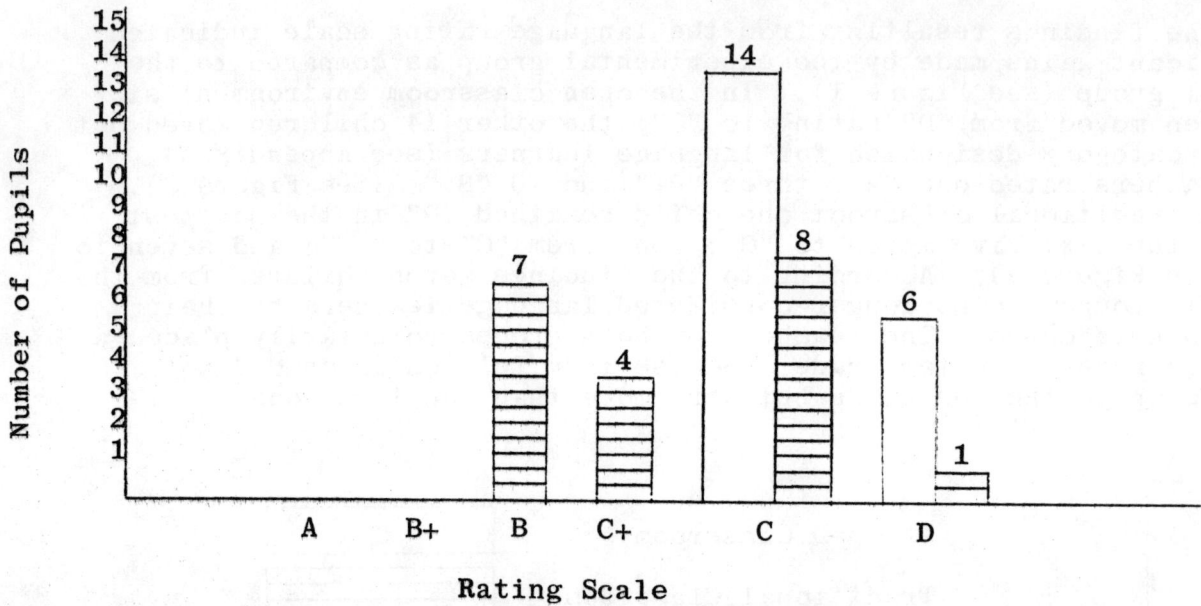

Figure 2. A histogram depicting the results of the Oral Language Rating Scale for the traditional classroom (n = 20).

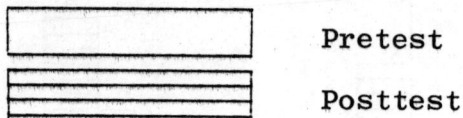

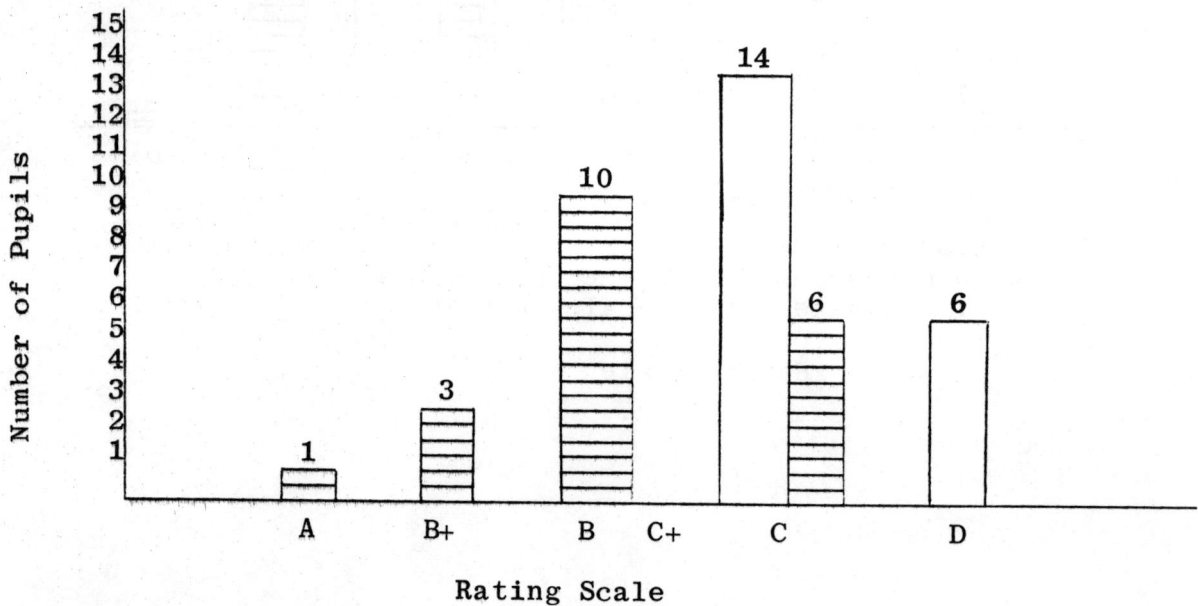

Pretest

Posttest

15
14
13
12
11
10
9
8
7
6
5
4
3
2
1

Number of Pupils

1

3

10

14

6

6

A   B+   B   C+   C   D

Rating Scale

Figure 3. A histogram depicting the results of the Oral Language Rating Scale for the open classroom pupils (n = 20).

50

How did second language learners in the fourth grade grow cognitively in the open classroom?

Flexible scheduling within the school day provided children the opportunity to work in pairs, in groups, or as individuals working independently of the teacher. Children enhanced their own learnings by becoming active participants in the learning process. Rather than being punished for bringing in materials from home, children were encouraged to contribute and to share these materials in the classroom. In one classroom two boys brought in a bird that had fallen out of a tree, and the children took turns nourishing it back to health. In the process of making kites in one classroom, the children brought in much of the personal decorations for their kites from home. Many ethnic materials, books, games, and records were on display which children either loaned or contributed permanently to the room. Self-directed activities were inspired by the variety of materials and/or discussions about the activities that were possible in further exploration of the materials. Children could be seen moving from ignorance to awareness as they acquired more knowledge about things that interested them or clarified life in their real world.

The "C" children, who generally needed to extend their vocabulary and refine their language usage skills to keep up with their peers, had many opportunities to do so in the open classroom setting. The second language learners acquired new words in a variety of ways - through communication with peers, accumulation of word charts and word lists, language games, flow charts, word association exercises, dictionaries, readings or labeling of objects.

The open classroom teachers were constantly providing experiences for children to reach their potential in all areas. Because they knew the needs of the children in the classroom, teachers planned learning strategies to help them develop cognitive skills characteristic of their cognitive styles. Language centered open classrooms increased the productive level of language as well as the reading as evidenced from the findings of the study. Children had wider interests in reading. Textbooks were found in the rooms, but more use was made of books about things or happenings found in the room. For instance, books about dinosaurs, gerbils, snakes, and a host of other subjects were popular in those classrooms exhibiting these things. More emphasis was placed on what to read and less on methodology for developing reading skills, although these skills were dealt with at times other than reading enjoyment time. Children's curiosity led them to seek more information to satisfy their own learning desires which they often expressed to their peers or to the teacher. Reading appeared to be more of a pleasure and less of a chore. There appeared to be a high correlation between linguistic and cognitive competencies. The results of this study showed a high correlation between the productive level of language and the ability to read.

Standardized tests measure only one phase of language-reading. Other language assessment instruments are less developed even though the productive level has been judged to be very essential to the reading level. Cloze reading tests measure many aspects of language in the process of assessing reading comprehension. Teachers may learn much about the productive level of children by analyzing the errors made in taking a Cloze reading test.

On the Cloze Reading Test used in this study, 27 words appeared in the noun position, 12 words in the verb position of which two were in the conditional tense and the rest in the past, two in both the adjective and the adverbial positions, and seven words were prepositions. All of these words had to be placed in sentences reconstructing a story that made sense to the reader. The sentence patterns used in the selection were relatively simple as:

Noun Position ⟶ Verb Position ⟶ Object of Verb

determiners	auxiliary	nouns
modifiers	clusters	adjectives
clusters		adverbs

Questions, statements and quotations were used in the story. Noun determiners such as the, some, one, this and my seemed to help the language learners place a noun word in the blank immediately following these determiners. Some of the nouns required the plural form. In some cases where students substituted another word that made sense in the story, they used a plural form indicating knowledge of a rule about plurals.

Original word	Substitution
nights	days, times
boys	friends, kids, children, people

Apostrophes were left out of words like Edward's or Peter's.

Children had learned that verbs denoted action taking place and often substituted another verb in the space provided.

Original word	Substitution
sleep	go, eat, read, play
is	was
had	have
sick	gone
asked	said

Contractions created problems for the language learners. The contracted word in the sentence "That's when he looks for you" received a zero score from both groups in the pre- and posttest. "I'll" in the sentence "I'll play with you" received two points (one person getting it right in both groups in the pre- and posttest). The following expressions containing the missing words underlined gave the most difficulty; for example:
1. He had no one to play with but his dog.
2. Sometimes after school, Peter would go to Edward's house for cookies.
3. He won't be going to school.
4. Do you get lonely when I'm at school?
5. He asked his dog.
Children also made substitutions with prepositions replacing one with another.

Original word	Substitution
to	at
in	at

Textbooks contain many time-related expressions requiring the reader to fully understand in order to comprehend a story. In this particular reading selection some of many such expressions appeared:

1. When they were little
2. All day
3. One day
4. Next day, morning
5. Some nights
6. Sometimes
7. After school
8. Afternoon
9. One morning
10. When I'm at school
11. When you were sick
12. This morning
13. All afternoon

The experimental group showed a significant increase in its decoding skills from the pretest to the posttest. Although the traditional group showed an increase in the posttest over the pretest, the gains were relatively insignificant. It was the children in the experimental group that made substitutions of words to complete the story.

Fifty-three percent or more on the test indicated an independent reading ability or competent level; 44 percent to 52 percent the instructional level; and below 44 percent the frustration level. In the open classroom 10 children were reading at the independent level on the pretest and 15 on the posttest. Four students were at the frustration level on the pretest and one on the posttest.

In the traditional classroom, seven children scored at the competent level on the pretest and the same on the posttest. One child was at the teachable level on the pretest and four on the posttest. Twelve children scored at the frustration level on the pretest and nine on the posttest. This information could be significant to classroom teachers who might be interested in diagnosing reading abilities or disabilities.

Portrait of a Second Language Learner

A closer study was made on one Spanish speaking girl, born in the United States but of Puerto Rican descent, because she exhibited anxieties in wanting to read the story selected for the Cloze test (see Appendix B), and because she was visibly frustrated at the task of filling in missing words during the pretest period. An interview with the teacher about her inability to complete the test revealed a picture of Lisa (not her real name) unlike what was perceived initially by the investigator. The teacher described her as lazy, stubborn, and slow academically. During the course of the study, Lisa did not display any of these characteristics in the presence of the investigator. On the contrary she was pleasant, concerned about her work, and anxious to read with anyone who had the time to hear her read.

Lisa was one of the children in this study who were developing reading skills in this free environment. Although born in the United States, Lisa was considered shy and reluctant to speak English in her primary grades. But this was not the picture of Lisa in the fourth grade. She was aggressive, talkative, and anxious to succeed. Lisa was experiencing her second year in an open classroom where according to the teacher this atmosphere released Lisa's learning potential. In fact, the teacher had higher expectations of Lisa and felt the need to direct Lisa's verbosity and aggression toward other areas of interest in the classroom. She was concerned about Lisa's stubbornness which was viewed as laziness. But in reality Lisa's interest was to succeed in reading primarily. She had to be encouraged to do other tasks.

Lisa's mother described her as a spoiled child generally having her own way at home, because she was the only girl amidst three older brothers. The interview with Lisa's mother revealed interesting facts about Lisa at home. She was described as very talkative about school, her teacher, her peers, her work, and any other school related events. She never wanted to stay home and never had to be prodded to get ready in the morning. She very often had to be reminded to do homework and on occasion asked for help. Lisa enjoyed making up stories, reading, writing, counting, singing, dancing, cooking, and doing other house-keeping chores. She spoke English at home the majority of the time. Her mother expressed contentment with Lisa's class placement and progress in the middle grades wishing she had had the opportunity to have been educated in such a free atmosphere.

Lisa's mother was born in Puerto Rico, had some schooling in the United States and was bilingual. Although she spoke English when the children were little, she wanted them to know Spanish as part of their heritage. Lisa, therefore, started public school knowing no English. Because of her early shyness and her class placement, she did not grasp the English language well enough to succeed in reading. Her capabilities of reading with fluency were diminished by her lack of essential skills in communication and comprehension. However, she was assigned a peer tutor in her class whose job it was to help Lisa improve those linguistic skills necessary to reach greater independence in reading.

The lessons used were culled from known texts in ESL, rexographed with very specific directions for the tutor on one sheet and the tutee on another, and distributed to the pairs. Although the children were trained to use the materials in a certain way, the tutors used their own initiative and intuition to develop techniques to help their partners. Lisa apparently gained from these sessions as indicated by her reading test scores and observed by her linguistic progress in the classroom and recorded on the language rating posttest. Lisa moved from a "C" rating (student who speaks English hesitantly at times, or whose regional or foreign accents indicate the need for remedial work in English and/or speech) to a "B" rating (student who speaks English fluently for her age level, or with no severe foreign accent). In the pretest of the Cloze Reading test, Lisa scored 18 (frustration level) but 80 in the posttest, indicating competency in comprehending stories at that level of difficulty.

Lisa filled in all 50 blanks in the posttest as compared to 11 answered in the pretest. She showed a determination to complete her work even if it means altering sentences in the passage. She aggressively made changes of words or structure to satisfy the meaning of the sentence. Examples of Lisa's alterations follow.

Original Sentence	Lisa's Sentence
1. One day they (would) play at Edward's house.	1. One day they went to Edward's house.
2. When they got big, the (boys) went to school.	2. When they got big, the They went to school.

54

Original Sentence	Lisa's Sentence
3. That's too (bad).	3. That's too <u>lonely</u>.
4. "Do you get (lonely) when I'm at <u>school</u>?" he (asked) his dog.	4. "Do you get lonely when I'm at school?" he <u>walkt</u> his dog.

In sentence 1 only one word was permitted even though Lisa's sentence made sense. In sentence 2 she crossed out the word <u>the</u>, capitalized <u>they</u> to make a new sentence that was semantically appropriate. But again this was against the rules. In sentence 3 this expression had not become Lisa's, although many other children had no difficulty with the term. In sentence 4 Lisa used the past tense of a verb but misspelled the word. She brought her own experiences and perceptions to the story. She had not noticed that quotation marks indicated a dialogue was taking place in the form of a question and told by a third person. The various substitutions made by Lisa suggested that she had internalized some rules about the English language and attempted to think through her body of knowledge to make choices in completing the passage. Although she was capable of using the right form of most words, indicating the interlanguage process was in operation, she did not use apostrophe marks for Edward's or Peter's in her written work. Time-related expressions did not present a problem to Lisa at posttest time.

During the observation period, Lisa used typical socio-linguistic terms she had heard from her peer group as "I got a notebook" or "It's mines." She had developed fluency in speaking in English. Her vocabulary had become more colorful and enriched. Occasionally there was interference of the Spanish pronunciation or intonation pattern in her new language. By the end of the year Lisa was capable of using more extended patterns and more complex language in her everyday communication in class. Many parents who visited the classrooms as well as teachers noted this rapid acquisition of the second language by the children in the open classrooms.

The literature as well as the large number of studies previewed in Chapter II support the advantages all children have in a socialized environment that abounds with materials and personal freedoms to choose and use these materials while learning. But this study was the only one to measure oral language abilities as well as reading abilities of children learning English as a second language in the fourth grade. The statistical analysis of the findings has, as predicted, confirmed the initial hypotheses that the language learner would increase his ability to comprehend in reading, and that the posttest scores would reflect a significant difference in the language learners in the open classroom as compared to those in the control group in the traditional classroom.

CHAPTER V

SUMMARY, CONCLUSIONS, AND RECOMMENDATIONS

Summary

Introduction

A summary of the investigation including its findings is presented in this chapter. The conclusions reached as a result of the investigation, recommendations based on the findings, and suggestions for further research are also indicated.

Purpose of the Study

The major purpose of this study was to compare second language acquisition in an open classroom environment with second language acquisition in a traditional environment. In addition, this study sought to ascertain the relationship of the findings and the answers to the following questions:

1. In what way does language instruction for the second language learner in the open classroom differ from the formal aural-oral language instruction given in traditional classrooms?

2. What is the relationship between the organizational plan of the open classroom and the achievement of communicative competence and linguistic competence?

3. What are the differences in achievement between the two groups from the pretests to the posttests of the New York City Language Rating Scale and a Cloze reading test?

4. How did second language learners in the fourth grade grow cognitively in the open classroom?

Design of the Study

The population for this study consisted of 40 fourth grade second language learners in New York City public schools rated "C or D" in their ability to speak English based on the New York City Language Rating Scale. "C" and "D" rated students were students who spoke English hesitantly at times, or whose regional or foreign accents indicated the need for remedial work in English and/or speech, and students who spoke only some stereotype sentences which they had been taught whose regional or foreign accents indicated the need for remedial work in English or speech. Twenty of these children were in five open classrooms in four schools in two school districts. Another 20 children were in three traditional classrooms in two schools in two schools in one school district. One traditional and one open classroom were located in the same school. All of the subjects were selected from ethnically integrated classrooms where English and other languages were spoken (Spanish, French, Chinese, and Thai).

The materials used to collect the data consisted of a language rating scale designed to rate pupil's ability to speak in English (see Appendix A). The children's speaking proficiency was rated on the scale by the classroom teacher in the open classroom or by the teacher of English as a Second Language (TESL) in the traditional classroom based upon the teacher's judgment of the children's oral structural patterns, vocabulary, intonation patterns, pronunciation, and comprehension demonstrated in conversations with the children.

A Cloze reading test (see Appendix B) was used to determine the readability and comprehension level of the students. This test had been found to be reliable with second language learners because it tested the whole process of reading (creativity, intelligence, concept development, and thinking); it considered use of words (functional or content); and it permitted guessing because of the redundancy of the English language.

Every sixth word was deleted from a reading selection which had 50 blanks. The children were given two points for filling in each blank with an appropriate word that made sense in the passage. Spelling errors were not counted against the students.

The reading passage was selected from Holt, Rinehart and Winston's Basic Reading System entitled A Time for Friends. The story "Two Friends" reflected an integral part of the home, school, and community with which the children were familiar. The selection was from level eight of the 12 levels comprising the basic primary language arts skills.

A teacher's questionnaire was used to determine the educational background of the teacher, the program, and the children in the class. It also sought to determine materials available or ordered, and how selected for effective instruction in the classroom. Finally it sought information about parent-teacher relationships within the school, the classroom, and the program (see Appendix C).

A screening and placement form was used to acquire information about each child's birthplace, age, sex, language spoken at home, previous schooling, present school placement and attendance patterns (see Appendix D).

A parent interview form (see Appendix E) was used to determine children's learning interests and abilities in reference to school and home. Collection of the above data was initiated in October of 1974 and completed in May of 1975.

For purposes of analysis, the following tests were designed:
1. The t test for independence was used to determine if there was a significant difference in the scores of the posttests on the Cloze reading test between the open classroom pupils and the traditional. The Hays Estimate measure was used to determine the relationship of the open classroom atmosphere and the significantly increased achievement of the children.
2. A correlated t test was used to determine significant differences in achievement from pretest to posttest for the two groups studied.
3. A covariance F test was used to determine significant differences in achievement between the open classroom pupils and the traditional classroom pupils. This test was used to offset differences in achievement attributable to the differences at the initial level.

Findings of the Study

The following are the major findings of the study:
In answer to question 1, language instruction for second language learners in open classrooms differed from the formal aural-oral language instruction given in traditional classrooms in many ways. The free atmosphere of an open classroom provided the human and environmental input needed to motivate the process of acquiring a second language at

the oral productive level and the graphic receptive level. The relationships among the teachers, the children, the curriculum, and the parents were different in the open classroom.

With respect to the teachers in the open classroom, all of them had been trained in open education philosophy but not in the methodology of English as a second language. The teachers shifted roles throughout the day alternating as mother, nurse, psychologist, counselor, teacher, and most of all facilitator in dealing with individuals. Although there were freedoms of choice, movement and expression, the classrooms were highly structured indicating a high degree of planning, evaluating, and record keeping. The teachers focused on the needs of the children in a child centered room.

With respect to the children and to Lisa in particular, a Spanish speaking child, all of them grew linguistically and cognitively in their own classroom environment. Separate language lessons were not provided for these fourth grade "C and D" rated pupils. Instead they acquired their second language through a combined interrelationship involving materials and peers. Language developed in coordination with sensori-motor behaviors. Children had ideas to express in the process of touching animals, plans, objects and instructional materials.

In the primary grades Lisa was considered shy and reluctant to speak English. She entered the school speaking no English. Her inability to grasp the English language in the early grades hindered her progress in reading. However, Lisa scored from "C to B" on the language rating scale and from 18 to 80 percent on the Cloze reading test indicating competency in the comprehension of the reading passage. Lisa filled in 50 blanks in the posttest as compared to 11 on the pretest. The many substitutions she made in filling in the answers suggested the interlanguage process in learning a second language was influencing her thoughts. Lisa, like most of the other children, left out apostrophe marks used in contractions. Progress was rapid and by the end of the school year, she was using more complex language in her everyday communications and a variety of socio-linguistic terms patterning the language of her social setting.

With respect to the curriculum, the learning centers housing available commercial, teacher, and pupil made materials indicated the diversity of the curriculum through which learning took place. Children developed from ignorance to awareness, from the known to the unknown, from fantasy to reality, and from incompetence to competence when involved with this abundance of learning materials. In fact more materials were always needed to challenge children to progress at their own levels of interests and abilities.

With respect to the parents, all of them were aware of the open classroom placement for their children having given the schools the permission to place the children in this individualized setting. The majority of the parents indicated on the questionnaire that the children enjoyed going to school to meet their friends, often initiated conversations about their work, classmates and teachers; did not have to be coaxed to get up for school; and never wanted to stay home.

In answer to question 2, the organizational plan in the open classroom did help the second language learners achieve communicative competence because freedom of speech in an interaction process gave the necessary opportunities to achieve verbal fluency as children used active and passive sentences, asked questions, gave commands, changed tenses, and used more complex transformational skills or figurative expressions in conversing with their peers or their teachers. Children were provided many opportunities to improve their skills through a variety of tasks to be performed on a one-to-one basis, by pairs or by groups in the learning centers.

Children had opportunities for developing their own cognitive and linguistic competencies in a facilitating environment offering physical, emotional and social involvement. Teachers and children shared the responsibilities of learning and teaching. Errors made in the process of language development were often self-corrected or quickly changed by peers or teachers.

In answer to question 3, the differences between the two groups on the pretest and posttest scores of the reading test were very significant. In the analysis of the data, comparisons were made between the achievement levels on the posttest scores of the two groups and a comparison of the achievement levels within each group's pretest and posttest scores. The sampling of 20 children in each group could receive a perfect score of 100 or the lowest score of 0. The posttest mean for the open classroom pupils was 72.2 from a range 36 to 94 with a standard deviation of 14.53 as compared to the posttest mean for the traditional classes which was 40.3 from a range of 2 to 74 with a standard deviation of 26.39. The difference in mean scores was 31.9 which when transformed to a t statistic was $t = 4.75$. This was significant at the .01 level. Hays estimate (W^2) was also used to determine how much of the increase was associated with the open classroom approach. This yielded a value of .35 which meant that the open classroom environment appeared to account for 35 percent of the obtained score.

The pretest mean for the open classroom pupils was 59.3 from a range of 18 to 92 and the posttest mean was 72.2, an increase in achievement of 12.9 points. This 12.9 difference in the mean grades was converted to a correlated t statistic ($t = 3.11$). This 3.11 was significant at the .01 level, which indicated a significant increase in achievement from the pretest to the posttest scores.

The pretest mean for the traditional classroom pupils was 34.6 from a range of 0 to 78, and the posttest 40.3, an increase of 5.7 points in achievement. This difference in mean grades converted to a correlated t statistic ($t = 1.92$) was not significant statistically even though there was some increase in the grades of the pupils from the pretest to the posttest.

By taking into account any initial difference in achievement (pretest scores) and posttest results between the groups, the F value for the analysis of covariance (anacova) was calculated to be 11.18, which is statistically significant at the .01 level. This analysis implied that the achievement for the pupils in the open classroom was significantly higher than the achievement for the pupils in the traditional classroom.

The findings resulting from the language rating scale indicated significant gains made by the experimental group as compared to the control group (see Figure 1). In the open classroom environment, six children progressed from "D to C" rating (see Figure 3); the other 14 children were no longer designated as language learners, having the verbal fluency of a native English speaker.

In the traditional classroom one child out of six remained at the "D" level; five moved from "D to C"; four from "C to C+"; and seven to "B" (see Figure 2). According to the findings, seven pupils reached the verbal fluency of native English speakers.

In answer to question 4, fourth grade language learners in a language centered environment progressed more rapidly linguistically and cognitively in this setting in comparison to the children in the traditional classroom. The study showed high correlations between linguistic competence and cognitive competence as well as between the productive level of language and the ability to read. The children in the open classroom made significantly more progress in the encoding and decoding skills in language.

Language universals having a predictive relationship between the noun and the verb (N.V.O.) appeared throughout the Cloze reading selection. In the noun position, determiners, modifiers, and clusters were included. In the verb position, auxiliary verbs and clusters were used in the passage. All that became the object of the verb, nouns, adjectives, and adverbs were evidenced. Questions, statements and quotations were other forms of language in the passage.

Of the 50 blanks representing missing words, 27 of them appeared in the noun position, 12 in the verb position of which two were in the conditional tense and the rest in the past tense, two in adjective and adverbial positions, and seven words appeared as prepositions. The open classroom pupils indicated that within their learning experiences the interlanguage process in second language learning was in operation. Children were internalizing some of the rules of the English language to help them fill in the missing words more effectively. Indications were that they were being creative in finding words that would fit the story.

Ten pupils in the open classroom were reading at the independent level on the pretest (over 53 percent score), six at the instructional level (44 percent to 52 percent), and four at the frustration level (under 44 percent). On the posttest 15 children scored at the independent level, four at the instructional level, and one at the frustration level.

In the traditional classroom, seven children scored at the competent level, one at the teachable, and 12 at the frustration level on the pretest. On the posttest, seven scored at the competent level, four on the teachable, and nine at the frustration level.

Conclusions

On the basis of the findings on the effectiveness of the open classroom climate on second language acquisition, the following conclusions were drawn:

1. In the open classroom environment where learning and teaching are shared in an atmosphere of informality and creativity, second language learners can acquire language and develop their cognitive skills more rapidly and more naturally than in a traditional setting.

2. Teachers can learn much about the productive level of students through careful analysis of Cloze reading tests.

3. Children, in this study, rated "C" on the New York City Language Rating Scale acquired their linguistic competencies well enough to be considered and treated as native speakers of English.

4. Fourth graders rated "D" on the scale increased their verbal fluency; used the stress, pitch, and rhythm of English showing only occasional interference of their own native language; gained automatic control of English pronunciation except for occasional interference of their own native pronunciation.

5. Making errors in the process of imitating or practicing a second language in the open classroom was a natural and necessary first step toward building language skills.

6. The open classroom environment can provide constant encoding and decoding practices children need to enhance their reading skills and broaden their cognitive base. The children in this study made

significant gains in reading not only as a result of their language ability; but because of their interests and personal motivation.

7. Opportunities for the second language learner to grow emotionally, socially, linguistically, and intellectually can be expected in the same manner that all children grow in an atmosphere in which individualization is an instructional goal as well as a basic educational principle.

Recommendations

The following recommendations, formulated directly from the findings and conclusions in this investigation, suggest possible courses of action and the need for further study:

1. Since second language learners made significant language gains at the productive and receptive levels in the processes of socializing, individualizing, sharing, exploring, problem solving, and manipulating materials, supervisors should examine their placement policies and the possibilities of second language learners maximizing their language learning potential in such a rich environment.

2. Since children in the open classroom were free to converse with peers in two language sharing other cultures, and since the literature on language acquisition indicated children were biologically capable of learning languages easily up through the middle grades, they should be provided the opportunity to learn those languages from teachers who are native speakers of the language in an arrangement where flexible scheduling is provided to focus on specific educational needs.

3. Since second language learners grew linguistically and cognitively in the open classroom environment with teachers who were provided special training in child development theories, teacher training institutions should offer training based upon child development theories and theories of second language acquisition for elementary school teachers at the preservice and inservice levels.

4. Since the productive level of language is so necessary to the receptive level of development, more research is needed to assess second language progress at the productive level or just how children develop the ability to produce oral language and continue to achieve fluency in that language.

5. Since the sampling in this study was small and there are so many variables in testing language acquisition, additional research is recommended involving a larger sampling of second language learners in similar open education classroom models in a variety of other geographic areas in the United States and/or in other parts of the world.

APPENDIX A

SCALE FOR RATING PUPIL'S ABILITY TO SPEAK ENGLISH

Puerto Rican Study
Board of Education, City of New York

"C" Students who speak English hesitantly at times, or whose regional or foreign accents indicate the need for remedial work in English and/or speech.

"D" Students who speak only some sterotype sentences which they have been taught whose regional or foreign accents indicate the need for remedial work in English or speech.

"A- Students who speak English Fluently for their age levels, or with
 B" no severe foreign accents. This group will contain students whose native languages are English, Spanish, French, or any other foreign languages.

"E- Students who speak little or no English, or whose regional or
 F" foreign accents make it impossible or almost impossible for them to be understood.

Please note: The above classification is based on the student's demonstrated ability to speak and understand English; not on his ability to read English.

APPENDIX B

CLOZE READING TEST

Name: _____

School: _____

Grade: _____

Room: _____

Read the story below. Fill in the blanks with a word that makes sense in the story. I will do the first and second blanks with you. Spell words the best you can. Spelling will not count.

Two Friends[+]

Annie Moorecroft.

Edward and Peter were old _____. When they were little, they _____ all day.

One day they _____ play at Edward's house. The _____ day they would play at _____ house.

Some nights Edward would _____ at Peter's house. And some _____ Peter would sleep at Edward's _____.

When they got big, the _____ went to school. At School _____ played and worked like old _____. Peter would read to Edward. _____ would read to Peter.

Sometimes _____ school, Peter would go to _____ house for cookies. Sometimes they _____ go to Peter's house.

Peter's _____ would have apples for the _____.

People said that Peter and _____ were like brothers.

One morning _____ went to Peter's house.

Peter's _____ came to the door,

"Peter _____ sick, "She said. "He won't _____ going to school."

"That's too _____" said Edwards. Edward went to _____ alone. He played with some _____.

He looked at pictures with _____.

But it was a bad _____ for Edward. He was lonely. _____ wanted to be with Peter.

63

_____ school Edward went home. He _____ no one to play with _____ his dog.

"Do you get _____ when I'm at school?" he _____ his dog.

"He gets lonely _____ the afternoon," said Edwards's mother.

"_____ when he looks for you. _____ wants you to come home. "_____ play with you," said Edward.

"_____ won't have to be lonely."

_____ played with his dog all _____.
But it was a lonely _____.

He wanted to be with _____ too.

The next morning Edward _____ to Peter's house. Peter came _____ the door.

"I'm all right _____ morning." he said.

"I'm going _____ school."

"That's good," said Edward.

"_____ was lonely when you were _____"

"We can play at my _____ after school." said Peter.

"No, _____ Edward.

"We have to go _____ my house. Then we can _____ with my dog. He gets lonely too."

+   Taken from a textbook

    Evertts, Hunt and Weiss
    A Time for Friends.'
    New York: Holt, Rinehart and Hinston, Inc.,
        1973 p 29-34

APPENDIX C

TEACHER QUESTIONNAIRE

1. How long have you been teaching?

_____

2. How much previous experience at this grade level?

_____

3. Have you taught children in disadvantaged areas?

_____

4. What degrees do you have? What specialty?

_____

5. What training have you had for 1. ESL?
                                   2. Open Classroom?

_____
_____

6. What courses have you had in 1. ESL Field?
                                2. Open Classroom?

_____
_____
_____

7. What additional training would you like to have?

_____
_____
_____

8. How does this program compare to any other you know?

_____
_____
_____

9. How do you feel about the program (the second language learner in
   the open classroom)?

_____
_____
_____
_____

10. What are the objectives of the open classroom for the second
    language learner?

    _____
    _____
    _____
    _____
    _____
    _____

11. What would you suggest to improve the program?

    _____
    _____
    _____
    _____
    _____
    _____

12. What is the student make-up in your class?
    Age_____   Sex _____   ESL _____
    Speak Spanish_____   Speak French _____   Other _____

13. What are the advantages of the program for the teacher? the child?

    _____
    _____
    _____
    _____
    _____
    _____

14. What are the disadvantages of the program for the teacher? the
    child?

    _____
    _____
    _____
    _____
    _____
    _____

15. Would you recommend continuing the program? With what modifications?

    _____
    _____
    _____
    _____
    _____
    _____

For Teachers About Materials
  1. What materials are on hand?

    _____
    _____
    _____
    _____
    _____

2. What materials have been ordered but not yet received?

_____
_____
_____

3. What special materials have been ordered for this program?

_____
_____
_____

4. Are the materials adequate?

_____

5. What additional materials would you suggest?

_____
_____

6. Are the materials interesting to the children? What have you observed about the way they have received the materials?

_____
_____
_____
_____

7. Were you part of the selection of materials?

_____

For Teachers About Parent Involvement

1. Did parents have a choice in deciding about the involvement of their children in the open classroom?

_____

2. Are parents aware of the program and its objectives?

_____
_____

3. Were workshops conducted for parents to assist and guide children through their own awareness of the current program and the techniques?

_____

4. Did you provide for interaction of parents of different social classes and ethnic groups? If so, describe.

_____
_____
_____

5. Are parents developing closer relationships between their children and themselves through common understanding of the school and the learning process? If so, explain.

_____
_____
_____
_____

6. How do parents communicate the cultural and emotional aspects of the children's environment to teachers?

_____
_____
_____
_____

APPENDIX D

SCREENING AND PLACEMENT FORM

1. Name: a. Last_____ b. First_____ c. Middle_____
2. Date of First Appearance at School_____ a. What Grade_____
3. Official Assignment_____
4. Address: A. No. and St._____ b. Apt._____ c. Floor_____
5. Date of Birth_____ 6. Age_____ 7. Sex: B___ G___
   mo. day yr.
8. Place of Birth_____
   city, town or rural locale   country
9. Father's Name_____ 10. Place of Birth_____
   last   first
11. Mother's Maiden Name_____ 12. Place of Birth_____
13. Date of Placement in This Class_____
14. Living in U.S.:   15. Living in NYC
    Since _____Yrs.___ Mos.___   Since _____ Yrs.___ Mos._____
16. Age first enrolled in a school_____
17. Previous schooling: a. None–Some b. If any, where?

P.R._____	Town_____
N.Y.C._____	Other USA_____
Elsewhere_____	
	country

18. Details of Previous Schooling

Details of Previous Schooling	in PR	in NYC	in Other US	Elsewhere
a. Grades Attended				
b. Academic Record				
c. Attendance Record				

Adapted from the puerto Rican Study form, Board of Education of the City of New York.

PARENT INTERVIEWS

P.S._____ Grade _____

Child_____ Teacher _____

Direction: Please check one of the five categories that best describe
your child.   There is no right or wrong answer.

1.   Child starts discussion about school without being asked:

Never	Very Rarely	Some Times	Very Often	Always

2.   When the child talks about school without being asked, he (she)
talks about:

a.   The Teachers?

Never	Very Rarely	Some Times	Very Often	Always

b.   The other children?

Never	Very Rarely	Some Times	Very Often	Always

c.   His (her) work?

Never	Very Rarely	Some Times	Very Often	Always

d.   Special events?

Never	Very Rarely	Some Times	Very Often	Always

e.   Things in the classroom?

Never	Very Rarely	Some Times	Very Often	Always

f. Other

```
|_____|_____|_____|_____|_____|
Never    Very     Some     Very     Always
         Rarely   Times    Often
```

3. Child brings things home he has made in school:

```
|_____|_____|_____|_____|_____|
Never    Very     Some     Very     Always
         Rarely   Times    Often
```

4. Child enjoys showing things he made in school:

```
|_____|_____|_____|_____|_____|
Never    Very     Some     Very     Always
         Rarely   Times    Often
```

5. Child must be reminded to do homework (older children only).

```
|_____|_____|_____|_____|_____|
Never    Very     Some     Very     Always
         Rarely   Times    Often
```

6. Child asks for help in doing homework (older children only).

```
|_____|_____|_____|_____|_____|
Never    Very     Some     Very     Always
         Rarely   Times    Often
```

7. Child wants to stay home from school.

```
|_____|_____|_____|_____|_____|
Never    Very     Some     Very     Always
         Rarely   Times    Often
```

8. Child requires coaxing or prodding in order to get ready for school.

```
|_____|_____|_____|_____|_____|
Never    Very     Some     Very     Always
         Rarely   Times    Often
```

9. Which of the following school-related activities does your child like to do at home without being asked

    a. reading (or looking at books or flash cards)

Never	Very Rarely	Some Times	Very Often	Always

    b. writing (or copying)

Never	Very Rarely	Some Times	Very Often	Always

    c. counting

Never	Very Rarely	Some Times	Very Often	Always

    d. painting or coloring

Never	Very Rarely	Some Times	Very Often	Always

    e. making things with clay or other material

Never	Very Rarely	Some Times	Very Often	Always

    f. Singing songs

Never	Very Rarely	Some Times	Very Often	Always

    g. dancing

Never	Very Rarely	Some Times	Very Often	Always

    h. Telling about historical events, or trips

Never	Very Rarely	Some Times	Very Often	Always

    i. making up stories

Never	Very Rarely	Some Times	Very Often	Always

j.　block-building

```
 |_____|_____|_____|_____|_____|
  Never    Very    Some    Very    Always
          Rarely  Times   Often
```

k.　initiating and pretending

```
 |_____|_____|_____|_____|_____|
  Never    Very    Some    Very    Always
          Rarely  Times   Often
```

l.　going to library or museum

```
 |_____|_____|_____|_____|_____|
  Never    Very    Some    Very    Always
          Rarely  Times   Often
```

m.　house keeping chores

```
 |_____|_____|_____|_____|_____|
  Never    Very    Some    Very    Always
          Rarely  Times   Often
```

n.　Cooking

```
 |_____|_____|_____|_____|_____|
  Never    Very    Some    Very    Always
          Rarely  Times   Often
```

o.　telephone classmates to discuss school work

```
 |_____|_____|_____|_____|_____|
  Never    Very    Some    Very    Always
          Rarely  Times   Often
```

p.　other _____

_____

10.　Of the nine items listed which do you consider the most important to you? Rank in order of importance. 1 through 9. e.g. If (h) is the most important put the number 1 in the space provided.

　　　　　　　　　　　　　　　　　　　　　　　　RANK

a.　Ability to do work and learn by
　　himself (herself)　　　　　　　　　　　　_____

b.　Respect for himself (herself)
　　as a valued person　　　　　　　　　　　　_____

c.　Being sensitive to his (her) own
　　feelings and the feelings of others　　_____

d.　Getting along with other people.　　　　_____

e.　Basic skills such as reading,
　　writing, arithmetic　　　　　　　　　　　　_____

f. Enjoyment in creating and
    experiencing beautiful things   _____

g. Learning things which can be used
    in his (her) everyday life (e.g.)
    dressing, grooming, health habits, etc.)_____

h. Principles of good citizenship   _____

i. Obedience to authority.   _____

P.S._____ Grade_____

Child_____ Teacher_____

Direccion: Favor de marcar una de las cinco categorias que mejor
describe a su niño o niña. Cualquier contestación es
aceptable.

ENTREVISTAS DE LOS PADRES

1. El niño habla acerca de la escuela sin nadie preguntarle:

Nunca	Muy Raramente	Algunos Veces	Muy A Menudo	Siempre

2. Cuando el niño habla acerca de la escuela sin que se le pregunte,
él o ella habla sobre:

   a. Las Maestras?

Nunca	Muy Raramente	Algunos Veces	Muy A Menudo	Siempre

   b. Los otros niños?

Nunca	Muy Raramente	Algunos Veces	Muy A Menudo	Siempre

   c. Los trabajo?

Nunca	Muy Raramente	Algunos Veces	Muy A Menudo	Siempre

   d. Actividades especiales?

Nunca	Muy Raramente	Algunos Veces	Muy A Menudo	Siempre

   e. Objectos en el salón?

Nunca	Muy Raramente	Algunos Veces	Muy A Menudo	Siempre

   f. Otros Cosas?

Nunca	Muy Raramente	Algunos Veces	Muy A Menudo	Siempre

3. El niño trae a la casa materiales que él ha hecho en al escuela.

Nunca	Muy	Algunos	Muy	Siempre
	Raramente	Veces	A Menudo	

4. El niño se siente contento al enseñar el trabajo que él ha en al escuela

Nunca	Muy	Algunos	Muy	Siempre

5. Hay que recordarle al niño que haga la tarea de la escuela (niños mayores solamente)

Nunca	Muy	Algunos	Muy	Siempre
	Raramente	Veces	A Menudo	

6. El niño pide que le ayuden a hacer la tarea de la escuela (niños mayores solamente)

Nunca	Muy	Algunos	Muy	Siempre
	Raramente	Veces	A Menudo	

7. El niño quiere quedarse en la casa Y no ir a la escuela

Nunca	Muy	Algunos	Muy	Siempre
	Raramente	Veces	A Menudo	

8. El niño requiere persuación e incentivos para que se prepare para ir a la escuela.

Nunca	Muy	Algunos	Muy	Siempre
	Raramente	Veces	A Menudo	

9. ¿Cual de las siguientes actividades escolares su nino o nina le gusta hacer en la casa sin que se le requiera hacerlo?

   a. leer (o mirar los libros o tarjetas escritas)

Nunca	Muy	Algunos	Muy	Siempre
	Raramente	Veces	A Menudo	

b. escribir (o copiar)

Nunca	Muy Raramente	Algunos Veces	Muy A Menudo	Siempre

c. contar

Nunca	Muy Raramente	Algunos Veces	Muy A Menudo	Siempre

d. pintar o colorear

Nunca	Muy Raramente	Algunos Veces	Muy A Menudo	Siempre

e. Hace objetos de barro o otro material

Nunca	Muy Raramente	Algunos Veces	Muy A Menudo	Siempre

f. Cantar Canciones

Nunca	Muy Raramente	Algunos Veces	Muy A Menudo	Siempre

g. baila

Nunca	Muy Raramente	Algunos Veces	Muy A Menudo	Siempre

h. hablar sobre eventos historicos o paseos

Nunca	Muy Raramente	Algunos Veces	Muy A Menudo	Siempre

i. Inventar cuentos

Nunca	Muy Raramente	Algunos Veces	Muy A Menudo	Siempre

j. jugar a mormar edificos con bloques

Nunca	Muy Raramente	Algunos Veces	Muy A Menudo	Siempre

k. imitando a pretendiendo

Nunca	Muy Raramente	Algunos Veces	Muy A Menudo	Siempre

l. visitando la bibliotéca o el museo

Nunca	Muy Raramente	Algunos Veces	Muy A Menudo	Siempre

m. haciendo que haceres de la casa

Nunca	Muy Raramente	Algunos Veces	Muy A Menudo	Siempre

n. cocinar

Nunca	Muy Raramente	Algunos Veces	Muy A Menudo	Siempre

o. llamar a los compañeros de escuela para discutir el trabajo de la escuela.

Nunca	Muy Raramente	Algunos Veces	Muy A Menudo	Siempre

p. otro

Nunca	Muy Raramente	Algunos Veces	Muy A Menudo	Siempre

10. ¿Cual de este nueve detalles mencionados considera usted más importante? Ordenelos segun la importancia que tengan para usted. Del 1 al 9. Si (h) es el más importante para usted escriba el numero 1 en el espacio correspondiente

RANGA

a. Abilidad para trabajar y aprender individualmente
_____

b. Respeto personal como persona de valor
_____

c. Ser sensitivo a sus sentimientos y los sentimientos de otros
_____

d. Saber convivir con otras personas
_____

e. Habilidades bósicas tales come leer, escribir y aritmetica
_____

f. Goze en crear y experimentar
    los cosas bellas   _____

g. Aprender cosas que le ayudarán
    en su vida diaria tales como
    vestirse, peinarse, hábitos, de
    salud, etc.   _____

h. Principio de buen cuidadano   _____

i. Obediencia a la autoridad   _____

APPENDIX F

DESCRIPTION OF

Rating Scale of Pupils' Ability to Speak English

VOCABULARY

	NE	F	E	D	C	B	A
		0	1	2	3	4	5
Description:	A child who does not respond because his dominant language is other than English. Cannot speak any English	A child who does not produce language for other reasons	Language is limited to identification; however, these responses are basically erroneous and inappropriate labels	Responses mostly identification, yielding general labels and unclear function responses. Much searching for correct word, but does not always find it	Is able to identify "things" with concrete specific labels as well as general ones; is able to respond in terms of function, but can make few relationships	Responds in terms of identification and function adequately, is able to show relationships in language reproduction, appropriate for age level. **Probing is required**	Some as No. 4 but without probing
Examples:			*For example:* "bell" for apple "ear" for banana or mouth "bird" for cash register	*For example:* "food" or "fruit" but not kind "box" for register "thing," "it," or "stuff" but can't specify even with probing	*For example:* "to keep money in" "to weigh food" "money machine"	*For example:* "it would be fat like a pear with string bean legs" "because she's hungry." "She's his sister." "He's going to take them home"	

STRUCTURE

	NE	F	E	D	C	B	A
		0	1	2	3	4	5
Description:	A child who does not respond because his dominant language is other than English. Cannot speak any English	A child who does not produce language for other reasons	Limited to single word responses; relies on gesture to convey meaning	No control of common patterns; phrase responses; indiscriminate selection of tense and gender; omits important words; unable to express plurals or possessive appropriately	Disjunctive control of common patterns; frequent errors in plural formation, gender, tense selection or agreement, word order and possessives	Adequate control of common patterns; restricted use of complex patterns; minimal error in gender, tense selection, agreement, plurals, and possessives, appropriate for age level	Complete control of complexity and variety of patterns available to a native speaker, appropriate for age level
Examples:			*For example:* "nose" "apple" "money" "banana"	*For example:* "turned it" "eating them" "He hold it" "holding things"	*For example:* "He have legs" "Is taking them to home" "He have them in his house" "How many it cost?"	*For example:* He is taking them to his mother" "Because she asked him for one"	*For example:* "She's hungry, because she didn't have breakfast" "He's going to take them home to share with his other brothers and sisters"

PRONUNCIATION

	NE	F	E	D	C	B	A
		0	1	2	3	4	5
Criterion description:	A child who does not respond because his dominant language is other than English. Cannot speak any English	A child who does not produce language for other reasons	Habitual mispronunciation of English consonant and vowel sounds	Frequent mispronunciation of English consonant and vowel sounds	Occasional mispronunciation of English consonant and vowel sounds	Infrequent mispronunciation of English consonant and vowel sounds	Standard English pronunciation

INTONATION

	NE	F	E	D	C	B	A
		0	1	2	3	4	5
Criterion description:	A child who does not respond because his dominant language is other than English. Cannot speak any English	A child who does not produce language for other reasons	Total interference of a foreign language	Excessive interference of a foreign language	Frequent interference of a foreign language	Occasional interference of a foreign langue	Standard English Intonation

5

APPENDIX G

GLOSSARY

1. Bicultural - a term used simultaneously with bilingual meaning
knowing the history and the culture of two linguistic worlds.
2. Bilingual - a term used in education to describe the ability
of a speaker to speak two languages equally well or almost equally.
Bordie (1970) pointed out that "bilingual students have a dual matrix
situation in which the relation of capacity in one area of native
language matrix to the same area of the second lanugage matrix must
be considered." MacNamara (1967) and Savard (1968) have defined the
four basic skills of listening, speaking, reading, and writing into
various subskills and levels.
3. Distar (Directional Instructional System for Teaching
    Arithmetic and Reading) - a reading program designed for small
groups of children at a time and calling for the undivided attention of
the teacher for approximately 25 minutes. It was designed to train
disadvantaged children to pay strict attention to the teacher and
observe sequence of letter sounds for making words. The program is
rigid in nature and is therefore under criticism by child development
specialists.[1]
4. Interlanguage - is a term used to describe a learning process
which is seen as the learner's approximate system or the intermediate
stage between the source and the target language which results from
transfer of training strategies of communication, learning and over-
generalization. Richards (1972) in his abstract defined interlanguage
in these terms: "The concept of interlanguage provides a basis for
dialect and language variety description, because it considers rules
which are linguistic in origin - derivable from the mother tongue and
limited exposure to the target language - and social in origin -
derived from communication and learning strategies" (n.p.).
5. Lexical - is a term used to relate to words, word formatives
or the vocabulary of a language as distinguished from its grammatical
construction. The culture of a community influences the meanings of
vocabulary words.
6. Merrill Linguistic Readers - is a basic reading program that
is scientific in its structure. The program was constructed around
Fries' (1963) analysis of the structure and the spelling system of the
English language. This reading program grew out of a close collaboration of a linguistic scientist, a reading specialist and a master
teacher in 1966.
7. Morphology - a linguistic term used to describe word formation
in a language including inflection, derivation and compounding. It is
the smallest linguistic unit in a language that has meaning.
8. Open Court - is a foundation reading program designed to
correlate language arts programs drawing the best approaches to beginning reading through phonics. Most of the program is done with the
whole class.[2]
9. Phonetics - a term used to describe the study of sounds made
in spoken utterance as they are reproduced by the organs of speech and
as they register on the ear.

10.   _Phonology_ – a term used to describe the science of speech sounds including the history and the theory of sound changes in a single language or in two or more related languages considered together or for comparative reasons.

11.   _Syntax_ – a term used to describe an orderly arrangement of words to show relationships in a sentence or sentence structure.

FOOTNOTES

1.   This project was originated by C. Bereiter, a psychologist, and S. Englemann, a promotion man (1964). Chicago: Service Research Associates, 1969.

2.   Open Court "Foundation Program" was written by Ann Hughes, published in 1965 and modified in 1970. La Salle, Ill.: Open Court Publishers, 1970.

ANTHONY J. POLEMENI, PH.D.
DIRECTOR (ACTING)

APPENDIX H

LETTER OF PERMISSION

Miss Iona L. Anderson
1116 Willmehr Street
Brooklyn, N.Y. 11212

Dear Miss Anderson:

I am happy to inform you that your proposed study entitled,
"INNOVATIONS IN THE USE OF THE OPEN CLASSROOM: THE FACILI-
TATING EDUCATIONAL ENVIRONMENT AND ITS IMPLICATIONS FOR THE
NATURAL ACQUISITION OF A SECOND LANGUAGE" has been approved
by the Office of Educational Evaluation, with the following
conditions:

1. Before involving any child in your study,
    you must obtain written parental consent.
    (I have enclosed a form which you may
    follow in drawing up your own Parental
    Permission Form).

2. Your report of the study should not include
    identification of any school personnel. A
    code system should be used.

3. You must make it very clear to your pros-
    spective respondents that their cooperation
    is on a purely voluntary basis.

Whenever your report is ready, I should be interested in re-
ceiving a copy.

Best wishes in this endeavor.

Sincerely yours,

Anthony J. Polemeni
Director (Acting)

AJP:WEW:1b
Enc:

P.S. You may duplicate this letter in any quantity you need in
     order to inform cooperating principals and community sup-
     erintendents that you have received approval from the
     Office of Educational Evaluation.

BIBLIOGRAPHY

About reading. In The learning cooperative: Supplement to learning in New York. New York: The Learning Cooperative, 1974-1975.

Allen, D. What the future of education might be. In T. Hipple (Ed.), The future of education: 1975-2000. Pacific Palisades, Calif.: Goodyear Publishing Co., Inc., 1974.

Allen, H.B. Teaching English as a second language: A book of readings. New York: McGraw-Hill, 1965.

Allen, J. Cited in A. Gentry, B. Jones, C. Peele, R. Phillips, J. Woodbury, & R. Woodbury, Urban education the hope factor. Philadelphia: Saunders, 1972.

Anderson, V., Anderson, P., Ballantine, F., & Howes, V. (Eds.). Reading in the language arts. New York: Macmillan Company, 1964.

Aristotle. Cited in B. Rosen, Philosophic systems and education. Columbus, Ohio: Charles Merrill Publishing Co., a Bell & Howell Co., 1968.

Aukerman, R. Approaches to beginning reading. New York: John Wiley & Sons, Inc., 1971.

Baker, J., Ross, J., & Walters, B. Each one learning. San Bernadino, Calif.: Regional Project Office, 1971.

Barker, V.D. Breakthrough to tomorrow. New York: United Nations, 1970.

Barth, R. Open education and the American school. New York: Agathon Press, Inc., 1972.

Bausch, R. The parent-teacher partnership. Reston, Va.: Council for Exceptional Children, Inc., 1969.

Been, S. Reading in the foreign language teaching program. TESOL Quarterly, 1975, 9, 223-242.

Berg, P.C., & Spache, G.D. The art of efficient reading (2nd ed.). New York: Macmillan, 1966.

Bergin, A., & Garfield, S. Handbook of psychotherapy and behavior change: Empirical analysis. New York: John Wiley & Sons, Inc., 1971.

Betancourt, R. Try the eclectic approach. Today's Education, September-October 1975, pp. 43-44.

Bever, T.G. The nature of cerebral dominance in speech behavior of the child and adult. In R. Husby & E. Ingram (Eds.), Language acquisition models and methods. New York: Academic Press, 1971.

Bever, T.G. Perceptions, thought and language. In R.O. Freedle & J.B. Carroll (Eds.), Language comprehension and the acquisition of knowledge. Washington, D.C.: V.H. Winston & Sons, 1972.

Bever, T.G., & Langendoen, D.T. A dynamic model of the evolution of language. Linguistic Inquiry, 1971, 2, 433-463.

Blackburn, R. English for foreign students goes out on the streets. TESOL Quarterly, 1971, 5, 251-260.

Blitz, B. The open classroom: Making it work. Boston: Allyn & Bacon, Inc., 1973.

Bloomfield, L. Language. New York: Henry Holt & Company, 1933.

Bordie, J. Language tests and linguistically different learners: The sad state of the art. Elementary English, 1970, 47, 817.

Bouton, L. Meeting the needs of children with diverse linguistic and cultural backgrounds. Speech delivered at TESOL Convention, Los Angeles, 1975.

Brameld, T. Workers' education in the United States. New York: Harper & Brothers, 1941.

Brameld, T. The remaking of a culture, life and education in Puerto Rico. New York: Harcourt & Brace, 1959.

Brameld, T. Motivation and personality (2nd ed.). New York: Harper & Row, 1970.

Braun, C. (Ed.). Language, reading and the communication process. Newark, Del.: International Reading Association, 1971.

Bremer, A., & Bremer, J. Open education: A beginning. New York: Holt, Rinehart & Winston, 1972.

Bremer, J., & von Moschzisker, M. The schools without walls. New York: Holt, Rinehart & Winston, Inc., 1971.

Bronfenbrenner on childhood. Behavior Today, 1975, 6, 447-448.

Brown, H.D. The psychological reality of grammar in the ESL classroom. TESOL Quarterly, 1972, 6, 263-269.

Brown, R. A first language: The early stages. Cambridge, Mass.: Harvard University Press, 1973.

Brown, R., & Bellugi, U. Three processes in children's acquisition of syntax. Harvard Education Review, 1964, 34, 133-151.

Brown, R., & Belluti, U. Cited in J. Ryan, Early language development. In M. Richards (Ed.), The integration of a child into a social world. New York: Cambridge University Press, 1974.

Brown, S. Adapting human relations training techniques for the ESOL classroom. Speech delivered at the TESOL Convention, Los Angeles, Calif., 1975.

Bruner, J. The process of education. New York: Vintage Books, a division of Random House, 1963.

Bruner, J. Toward a theory of instruction. Cambridge, Mass.: Belknap, 1966.

Bruner, J.S. Toward a theory of instruction (2nd ed.). Cambridge, Mass.: Harvard University Press, 1967.

Bruner, J. The act of discovery. In M. Silberman, J. Allender, & J. Yanoff, The psychology of open teaching and learning: An inquiry approach. Boston: Little, Brown & Co., Inc., 1972.

Bruner, J., Goodnow, J., & Austin, G. A study of thinking. New York: Science Editions, Inc., 1962.

Bugelski, B. The psychology of learning applied to teaching. Indianapolis, Ind.: Bobbs-Merrill Co., Inc., 1964.

Buswell, G.T. Fundamental reading habits: A study of their development (Supplementary Educational Monographs, No. 21). Chicago: University of Chicago Press, 1922.

Campbell, R., & Wales, R. The study of language acquisition. In J. Lyons (Ed.), New horizons in linguistics. London: Allen Lane, 1970.

Carroll, J. Language, thought, and reality. Cambridge, Mass.: Institute of Technology Press, 1956.

Cazden, C.B. The acquisition of noun and verb inflections. Child Development, 1968, 39, 433-448.

Cazden, C. Child language and education. New York: Holt, Rinehart, & Winston, 1972.

Chavez, S. Preserve their language heritage. In V. Anderson, P. Anderson, F. Ballantine, & V. Howes (Eds.), Readings in the language arts. New York: Macmillan Company, 1964.

Chess, S., & Thomas, A. Annual progress in child psychiatry and child development. New York: Brunner/Mazel Publishers, 1970.

Child, I. Humanistic psychology and the research tradition: Their several virtues. New York: John Wiley & Sons, Inc., 1973.

Chomsky, N. Syntax structures. The Hague: Mouton, 1957.

Chomsky, N. Aspects of the theory of syntax. Cambridge, Mass.: MIT Press, 1965. (a)

Chomsky, N. The general properties of language. In F.L. Darley (Ed.), Brain mechanisms underlying speech and language (Proceedings

of a conference held at Princeton, N.J., November 9-12, 1965).
new York: Grune & Stratton, Inc., 1965. (b)

Chomsky, N. Cartesian linguistics: A chapter in the history of rationalist thought. New York: Harper & Row, 1966.

Chomsky, N. Language and mind. New York: Harcourt, Brace & World, Inc., 1968.

Chomsky, N. Cited in J. Lyons, Noam Chomsky. New York: The Viking Press, 1970.

Clark, D. Teaching concepts in the classroom: A set of teaching prescriptions derived from experimental research. Journal of Educational Psychology, 1971, 62, 253-278.

Clarke, A.C. Profiles of the future. New York: Bantam Books, Harper & Row Publishers, Inc., 1972.

Cohen, D. The learning child. New York: Vintage Books, Random House, 1972.

Collison, O. Concept formation in a second language: A study of Ghanaian school children. Harvard Educational Review, 1974, 44, 441-456.

Conger, S.D. Social inventions. Prince Albert, Canada: Saskatchewan Newstart, 1974.

Cremin, L. The Free School Movement. Today's Education, the Journal of the National Education Association, 1975, 64 (3), 71-74.

Croft, K. Readings on English as a second language. Massachusetts: Winthrop Publishing, Inc., 1972.

Dahlof, U. Trends in process-related research on curriculum and teaching of different problem levels in educational sciences. Scandinavian Journal of Educational Research, 1974, 18, 62-73.

DeCecco, J.P. The psychology of language, thought and instruction: Readings. New York: Holt, Rinehart & Winston, 1967.

DeChant, E. Improving the teaching of reading (2nd ed.). Englewood Cliffs, N.J.: Prentice-Hall, Inc., 1970.

Delgado, J. Physical control of the mind: Toward a psychocivilized society. New York: Harper & Row, Publishers, 1969.

Delgado, J. Cited in R. Restak, Exploring inner space. Saturday Review, August 9, 1975, pp. 21-25.

Dewey, J. How we think. New York: D.C. Heath & Company, 1933.

Dewey, J. School and society. New York: D.C. Heath & Company, 1956.

Dobzhansky, T. Mankind evolving: The evolution of the human species. New Haven, Conn.: Yale University Press, 1962.

Dulay, H., & Burt, M. You can't learn without goofing: An analysis of children's second language errors. 1972. (ERIC Document Reproduction Service No. ED 066 981)

Dulay, H., & Burt, M. Errors and strategies in child second language acquisition. Speech made at TESOL Convention, San Juan, P.R., March 1973.

Dulay, H., & Burt, M. Errors and strategies in child second language acquisition. TESOL Quarterly, 1974, 8, 129-135.

Durkin, K. Phonics, linguistics and reading. New York: Teachers College Press, Columbia University, 1972.

Eliot, J. Human development and cognitive processes. New York: Holt, Rinehart & Winston, 1971.

Elkind, D. We can teach reading better. Today's Education, NEA Journal, November-December 1975, pp. 34-38.

Erwin-Tripp, S. Structured process in language acquisition. In J.E. Alatis (Ed.), Twenty-first annual round table: Bilingualism and language contact. Washington, D.C.: Georgetown University Press, 1970.

Erwin-Tripp, S. Social dialects in developmental sociolinguistics. In R. Shuy (Ed.), Sociolinguistics: A cross-disciplinary perspective. Washington, D.C.: Center for Applied Linguistics, 1971.

Erwin-Tripp, S. Is second language learning like the first. TESOL Quarterly, 1974, 8, 111-127.

Faure, E., Felipe, H., Kaddoura, A-R., Lopes, H., Petrovsky, A., Rahnema, M., & Ward, F.C. Learning to be: The world of education today and tomorrow. London: United Nations, UNESCO, and George Harrup & Company, 1972.

Finocchiaro, M. English as a second language: From theory to practice. New York: Regents Publishing Company, Inc., 1964.

Finocchiaro, M. Learning to use English. New York: Regents Publishing Company, Inc., 1966.

Fishman, J. Sociolinguistics: A brief introduction. Rowley, Mass.: Newbury House Publishers, 1972.

Flavell, J.H. The developmental psychology of Jean Piaget. Princeton, N.J.: D. Van Nostrand Company, Inc., 1963.

Flavell, J., & Elkind, D. Studies in cognitive development: Essays in honor of Jean Piaget. New York: Oxford University Press, 1969.

Frank, M. From theory to practice: Situational reinforcement. New York: Institute of Modern Languages, 1974.

Friedl, B.C. Techniques in spoken language. Specific procedures in the ASTP foreign area and language studies. The Modern Language Journal, October 1944, pp. 476-498.

Fries, C. A new approach to language learning. New York: ELEC Publishers, 1960.

Fries, C. Linguistics and reading. New York: Holt, Rinehart & Winston, 1963.

Fuller, R. Buckminster. Utopia or oblivion: The prospects for humanity. New York: Bantam Books, 1969.

Furth, H. Piaget and knowledge: Theoretical foundations. Englewood Cliffs, N.J.: Prentice-Hall, Inc., 1969.

Gardner, R. Open end discussion: Reading for native Americans. New York Post, May 14, 1975.

Gartner, A., Kohler, M., & Riessman, F. Children teach children. New York: Harper & Row, Publishers, 1971.

Gattegno, C. Towards a visual culture: Educating through television. New York: Avon Books, 1969.

Gattegno, C. What we owe children: The subordination of teaching to learning. New York: Avon Books, 1970.

Gattegno, C. The adolescent and his will. New York: Outerbridge & Dienstfrey, 1971.

Gentry, A., Jones, B., Peele, C., Phillips, R., Woodbury, J., & Woodbury, R. Urban education the hope factor. Philadelphia: Saunders, 1972.

Ginsburg, H., & Opper, S. Piaget's theory of intellectual development: An introduction. New York: Prentice-Hall, 1969.

Gittler, J.B. Cultural pluralism in contemporary American society. International Journal of Group Tensions, 1974, 4, 322-343.

Glasser, W. Schools without failure. New York: Harper & Row, 1969.

Goodman, K. Readings: A psycholinguistic guessing game. International Reading Association Conference Papers, 1970, 14, 259-272.

Goodman, K. Effective teachers of reading know language and children. Elementary English, 1974, 51, 823-828.

Gordon, I.J. Human development: Readings in research. Chicago: Scott Foresman, 1965.

Grath, E. The time bomb of technocratic education. Change, the Magazine of Higher Learning, 1974, 6, 24-29.

Graubard, P., & Rosenberg, H. Classrooms that work: Prescriptions for change. New York: E.P. Dutton & Co., Inc., 1974.

Gross, R., & Gross, B. Will it grow in a classroom? New York: Delacorte Press, 1974.

Gumperz, J., & Hymes, D. Directions in sociolinguistics. New York: Holt, Rinehart & Winston, Inc., 1972.

Gunderson, D. Language and reading: An interdisciplinary approach. Washington, D.C.: Center for Applied Linguistics, 1970.

Gurth, H.P. English for a new generation. New York: McGraw-Hill Book Company, 1973.

Hall, E. The silent language. Garden City, N.Y.: Doubleday, 1959.

Hall, R., Jr. Linguistics and your language (2nd rev. ed.). Garden City, N.Y.: Anchor Books, Doubleday & Company, 1960.

Harrison, R. Beyond words: An introduction to nonverbal communication. Englewood Cliffs, N.J.: Prentice-Hall, Inc., 1974.

Hart, L. The neglected role of the brain in learning. K-Eight Instructional Management and Leadership, 1974, pp. 19-21.

Haskell, J. Selecting reading materials: A new approach. Idiom, 1972, 3, 1-3.

Havighurst, R. Human development and education. Chicago: University of Chicago, 1961.

Haynes, C. Humanizing instruction in the open classroom. Educational Horizons, 1973, 52, 32-35.

Hays, W.L. Statistics for psychologists. New York: Holt, Rinehart, & Winston, 1963.

Heidegger, M. Cited in W. Richardson, Heidegger through phenomenology to thought (2nd ed.). The Hague, Netherlands: Martinus, Nijhoff, 1967.

Hentoff, N. The future of education: Basic considerations. In T. Hipple (Ed.), The future of education: 1975-2000. Pacific Palisades, Calif.: Goodyear Publishing Company, Inc., 1974.

Hilgard, E. Theories of learning. New York: Appleton-Century-Crofts, Inc., 1956.

Hipple, T. (Ed.). The future of education: 1975-2000. Pacific Palisades, Calif.: Goodyear Publishing Company, Inc., 1974.

Hurlock, E. Child development (5th ed.). New York: McGraw-Hill Book Company, 1972.

Hymes, D. Cited in C. Cazden, Child language and education. New York: Holt, Rinehart & Winston, Inc., 1972.

Illich, I.D. Celebration of awareness. New York: Anchor Books, Doubleday & Company, Inc., 1971.

Illich, I. The breakdown of schools: A problem or a symptom? In T. Hipple (Ed.), The future of education: 1975-2000. Pacific Palisades, Calif.: Goodyear Publishing Company, Inc., 1974.

Inhelder, B., & Piaget, J. The growth of logical thinking from childhood to adolescence: An essay on the construction of formal operational structures. New York: Basic Books, 1958.

Jacobson, R. Cultural linguistic pluralism and the problem of motivation. TESOL Quarterly, 1971, 5, 265-285.

Jakobovits, L. On becoming a language teacher. TESOL Quarterly, 1972, 3, 206-212.

Jakobovits, L. Freedom to teach and freedom to learn. TESOL Quarterly, 1973, 7, 117-128.

James, W. Essays in radical empiricism - A pluralistic universe. New York: Longman's, 1943.

Johnson, R.C., & Medinnus, G.R. Child psychology - Behavior and development. New York: John Wiley & Sons, 1967.

Kaban, B., & Shapiro, B. How to raise a competent child. Harvard Magazine, July-August 1975, pp. 14-19.

Kallen, T.M. The education of free men: An essay toward a philosophy of education in America. New York: Farrar & Straus, 1949.

Kamii, C., & DeVries, R. Piaget-based curricula for early childhood education: Three different approaches. Philadelphia: Society for Research in Child Development, 1973. (ERIC Document Reproduction Service No. ED 087 518)

Kant, I. Cited in W. Richardson, Heidegger through phenomenology to thought (2nd ed.). The Hague, Netherlands: Martinus, Nijhoff, 1967.

Kerlinger, F. Research in education. In Encyclopedia of educational research (4th ed.). New York: Macmillan Co., 1969.

Kilpatrick, W. Modern education and better human relations. New York: ADL, 1949.

Klasson, F., & Imig, D. National and community needs: The challenge for teacher education. Washington, D.C.: ICET, 1973.

Kohl, H.R. The open classroom: A practical guide to a new way of teaching. New York: Random House, Inc., 1969.

Kostelanetz, R. Beyond left and right: Radical thought for our times. New York: William Morrow & Co., Inc., 1969.

Lado, R. Linguistics across cultures: Applied linguistics for language teachers. Ann Arbor: University of Michigan Press, 1961.

Lado, R. Language teaching: A scientific approach. New York: McGraw-Hill, 1964.

Lambert, W.E., Just, M., & Segalowitz, N. Some cognitive consequences of following the curricula of the early school grades in a foreign language. In J.E. Alatis (Ed.), Twenty-first round table: Bilingualism and language contact. Washington, D.C.: Georgetown University Press, 1970.

Lambert, W.E., Just, M., & Segalowitz, N. Cited in C. Cazden, Child language and education. New York: Holt, Rinehart, & Winston, 1972.

Langer, J. Theories of development. New York: Holt, Rinehart & Winston, 1969.

Lavatelli, C.S. A Piaget-derived model for compensatory preschool education. In I.J. Gordon (Ed.), Human development readings in research. Chicago: Scott Foresman, 1965.

Lavatelli, C.S. A Piaget-derived model for compensatory preschool education. In J. Frost (Ed.), Early childhood education rediscovered. New York: Holt, Rinehart & Winston, 1968.

Leedom, J. Linking up through links. American Education, August-September 1971, pp. 31-32.

LeFevre, C.A. Linguistics, English and the language arts. Boston: Allyn & Bacon, 1970.

Lenneberg, E.H. New directions in the study of language. Cambridge, Mass.: MIT Press, 1964.

Lenneberg, E.H. Biological foundations of language. New York: John Wiley & Sons, 1967.

Lenneberg, E. On explaining language: The development of language in children can best be understood in context of developmental biology. In S. Chess & A. Thomas (Eds.), Annual progress in child psychiatry and child development. New York: Brunner/ Mazel, 1970.

Lenneberg, E.H. Language and the brain: Developmental aspects. Neuro Sciences Research Bulletin, 1974, 12, 576-633.

Lifton, B. Why some preschoolers are ready to read before school. Parent's Magazine and Better Homemaking, March 1974, pp. 35-37.

Logan, L.M., Logan, V.G., & Paterson, L. Creative communication: Teaching the language arts. New York: McGraw-Hill, 1972.

Lyons, J. Noam Chomsky. New York: The Viking Press, 1970.

MacNamara, J. The bilingual's linguistic performance: A psychological overview. Journal of Social Issues, 1967, 23, 58-77.

Mayor's Committee on New Residents. A six month report on the Migration Services Department. Chicago: Chicago Commission on Human Relations, January 1958, April 1959.

McNeill, D. Developmental psycholinguistics. In F. Smith & G. Miller (Eds.), The genesis of language. Cambridge, Mass.: MIT Press, 1966.

McNeill, D. The acquisition of language: The study of developmental psycholinguistics. New York: Harper & Row, 1970.

McNeill, D. Acquisition of language: The study of developmental psycholinguistics (2nd ed.). New York: Harper & Row, 1972.

Malmstrom, J. Language in junior college: A socio-linguistic approach. (ERIC Document Reproduction Service No. ED 085 748)

Maslow, A. Higher and lower needs. Journal of Psychology, 1948, 25, 433-436.

Maslow, A. Toward a psychology of being (2nd ed.). Princeton, N.J.: Van Nostrand, 1968.

Maslow, A. Motivation and personality (2nd ed.). New York: Harper & Row, 1970.

Maslow, A.H. Defense and growth. In M. Silberman, J. Allender, & J. Yanoff (Eds.), The psychology of open teaching and learning: An inquiry approach. Boston: Little, Brown & Company, 1972.

Mathies, L. Cities on the educational horizon. Educational Horizon, 1974, 52, 153-160.

Milon, J. The development of negation in English by a second language learner. TESOL Quarterly, 1974, 8, 137-143.

Morrissett, I., & Stevens, W.W., Jr. Social science in the schools: A search for rationale. New York: Holt, Rinehart & Winston, Inc., 1971.

Mussen, P.H., Conger, J.J., & Kagan, J. (Eds.). Readings in child development and personality (2nd ed.). New York: Harper & Row, 1969.

New York City Board of Education, Office of Bilingual Education special study conducted by the Community Service Society of New York, August 1973.

Noar, G. Individualized instruction: Every child a winner. New York: John Wiley & Sons, Inc., 1972.

Norberg, K.D. Iconic signs. Sacramento, Calif.: Sacramento State College, 1966. (ERIC Document Reproduction Service No. ED 013 371)

Norris, D. The shape of schools to come. Parent Magazine and Better Homemaking, January 1975, pp. 40-44.

Nyquist, E.B., & Hawes, G.R. Open education: A sourcebook for parents and teachers. New York: Bantam Books, Inc., 1972.

O'Connell, V., & O'Connell, A. Choice and change: An introduction to the psychology of growth. Englewood Cliffs, N.J.: Prentice-Hall, Inc., 1974.

Oller, J. Transformational theories and pragmatics. Modern Language Journal, 1970, 54, 504-506.

Oller, J. Cloze tests of second language proficiency and what they measure. Language Learning, 1973, 23, 105-118.

Oller, J., & Inal, N. A Cloze test of English prepositions. TESOL Quarterly, 1971, 5, 315-322.

Pajestka, J. The social dimensions of development (United National Executive Briefing Paper 3). Geneva: United Nations, 1970.

Palmer, H. The teaching of oral English. London: Longman's Green & Company, 1940.

Pavlov, I. Conditioned reflexes. New York: Oxford University Press, 1927.

Paulston, C. Linguistic and communicative competence. TESOL Quarterly, 1974, 8, 347-362.

Piaget, J. The origins of intelligence in children. New York: International Universities Press, 1952.

Piaget, J. Play, dreams and imitation in childhood. New York: Norton, 1962.

Piaget, J. Cited in J.H. Flavell, The developmental psychology of Jean Piaget. Princeton, N.J.: D. Van Nostrand Company, Inc., 1963.

Piaget, J. The language and thought of the child. New York: World Publishing, 1965.

Piaget, J. Cited in I.J. Gordon, Human development: Readings in research. Chicago: Scott Foresman, 1965.

Piaget, J. Six psychological studies (trans. D. Elkins). New York: Random House, 1967.

Piaget, J. Cited in C.S. Lavatelli, A Piaget-derived model for compensatory preschool education. In J. Frost (Ed.), Early childhood education rediscovered. New York: Holt, Rinehart & Winston, 1968.

Piaget, J. Cited in H. Furth, Piaget and knowledge: Theoretical foundations. Englewood Cliffs, N.J.: Prentice-Hall, 1969.

Piaget, J. Cited in C. Kamii & R. DeVries, Piaget-based curricula for early childhood education: Three different approaches. Philadelphia: Society for Research in Child Development, 1973. (ERIC Document Reporduction Service No. ED 087 518)

Pike, K. The intonation of American English. Ann Arbor, Mich.: The University of Michigan Press, 1967.

Pike, K. Language relation to a unified theory of structure of human behavior. In P. Davis, Modern theories of language. Englewood Cliffs, N.J.: Prentice-Hall, Inc., 1973.

Plato. Cited in B. Rosen. Philosophic systems and education. Columbus, Ohio: Charles Merrill Publishing Company, A Bell & Howell Co., 1968.

Pollio, M., & Pollio, H. The development of figurative language in school children. Knoxville, Tenn.: Tennessee University, 1971. (ERIC Document Reproduction Service No. ED 087 524)

Postman, N., & Weingartner, C. Linguistics: A revolution in teaching. New York: Dell Publishing Company, Inc., 1966.

Postman, N., & Weingartner, C. Teaching as a subversive activity. New York: A Delta Book, Dell Publishing Company, Inc., 1969.

Puhl, C.A. A practical humanism for developing communicative competence in the ESL learner. Speech delivered at TESOL convention, Los Angeles, Calif., 1975.

Rankin, E. Cloze procedure - A survey of research. In The philosophical and sociological bases of reading, Fourteenth Yearbook of the National Reading Conference. Milwaukee: National Reading Conference, 1965.

Rebelsky, F., & Dorman, L. Child development and behavior: Readings (2nd ed.). New York: Alfred Knopf, Inc., 1973.

Reed, C.E. The pronunciation of English in the state of Washington. American Speech, 1952, 27, 186-189.

Reed, E. Improving comprehension through study of syntax and paragraph structure in seventh grade English classes. In C. Braun (Ed.), Language, reading and the communication process. Newark, Del.: International Reading Association, 1971.

Restak, R. Exploring inner space. Saturday Review, August 9, 1975, pp. 21-25.

Richards, J. Social factors, interlanguage and language learning. 1972. (ERIC Document Reproduction Service No. ED 066 966) (a)

Richards, J. Some aspects of language learning. TESOL Quarterly, 1972, 7, 243-251. (b)

Richards, M.P.M. (Ed.). The integration of a child into a social world. New York: Cambridge University Press, 1974.

Richardson, W. Heidegger through phenomenology to thought (2nd ed.). The Hague, Netherlands: Martinus, Nijhoff, 1967.

Rivers, W. Talking off the tops of their heads. TESOL Quarterly, 1972, 6, 71-82.

Rivers, W. From linguistic competence to communicative competence.
 TESOL Quarterly, 1973, 7, 25-34.

Rogers, C. Cited in M. Silberman, J. Allender, & J. Yanoff, The
 psychology of open teaching and learning: An inquiry approach.
 Boston: Little, Brown, & Company, 1972.

Rosen, B. Philosophic systems and education (Foundation of Education
 Series). Columbus, Ohio: Charles Merrill Publishing Company,
 1968.

Rosenbaum, P. Language instruction and the schools. In J. Alatis
 (Ed.), Monograph series on languages and linguistics, Number 22.
 Washington, D.C.: Georgetown University Press, 1970.

Ryan, J. Early language development. In M. Richards (Ed.), The
 integration of a child into a social world. London: Cambridge
 University Press, 1974.

Sapir, E. Language. New York: Harcourt, Brace, 1921.

Sapir, E. Language: An introduction to the study of speech. New York:
 Harcourt, Brace & World, 1949.

Sapir, E. Selected writings of Sapir in language, culture and personality. Berkeley, Calif.: Berkeley University Press, 1956.

Satir, V. Peoplemaking. Palo Alto, Calif.: Science & Behavior
 Books, Inc., 1972.

Savard, J. A proposed system for classifying language tests.
 Language Learning (special issue), 1968, No. 3, 167-174.

Senior, C. Strangers then neighbors: From pilgrims to Puerto Ricans.
 New York: Anti-Defamation League of B'nai B'rith, 1961.

Silberman, C.E. Crisis in the classroom: The remaking of American
 education. New York: Vintage Books, Random House, 1971.

Silberman, C.E. The open classroom reader. New York: Random House,
 1973.

Silberman, M., Allender, J., & Yanoff, J. (Eds.), The psychology of
 open teaching and learning - An inquiry approach. Boston:
 Little & Bacon, Inc., 1972.

Skinner, B.F. A case history in scientific method. American Psychologist, 1956, 11, 221-233.

Skinner, B.F. Verbal behavior. New York: Appleton, 1957.

Smith, F. Understanding reading: A psycholinguistic analysis of
 reading and learning to read. New York: Holt, Rinehart, &
 Winston, 1971.

Smith, F. Psycholinguistics and reading. New York: Holt, Rinehart &
 Winston, 1973.

Smith, W. Cited in C. Braun (Ed.), Language, reading and the communication process. Newark, Del.: International Reading Association, 1971.

Spolsky, B. Linguistics and language pedagogy - Applications or implications? In J. Alatis (Ed.), Monograph series on language and linguistics, Number 22. Washington, D.C.: Georgetown University Press, 1970.

Stauffer, R. The language experience approach to the teaching of reading. New York: Holt, Rinehart & Winston, 1970.

Stauffer, R. The quest for maturity in reading. In C. Braun (Ed.), Language, reading and the communication process. Newark, Del.: International Reading Association, 1971.

Stephens, J., & Evans, E. Development and classroom learning: An introduction to educational psychology. New York: Holt, Rinehart & Winston, Inc., 1973.

Stephens, L. The teacher's guide to open education. New York: Holt, Rinehart & Winston, Inc., 1974.

Stevick, E. Materials for the whole learner. Address delivered at forum on ESL materials for adults in CUNY, English Language Center, LaGuardia Community College, 1975.

Stoff, S., & Schwartzberg, H. The human encounter - Readings in education. New York: Harper & Row Publishers, 1969.

Taylor, B. Adult language learning strategies and their pedagogical implications. TESOL Quarterly, 1975, 9, 391-399.

Taylor, S.E. Eye movements in reading: Facts and fallacies. American Educational Research Journal, 1965, 2, 187-202.

Taylor, W. Cloze procedure: A new test for measuring readability. Journalism Quarterly, 1953, 30, 415-433.

Taylor, W. Present development on the use of the Cloze procedure. Journalism Quarterly, 1956, 33, 42-48.

Taylor, W. An introduction to the Cloze procedure. Newark, Del.: International Reading Association, 1972.

Thelen, H. Learning by teaching. Report of a conference on Helping Relationships in the Classroom, Stone-Brandel Center, University of Chicago, 1968.

Thomas, C. Phonetics of American English. New York: The Ronald Press Company, 1958.

Thonis, E. Teaching reading to non-English speakers. New York: The Macmillan Company, 1970.

Thornbury, R. Teachers' centres. New York: Agathon Press, 1974.

Thorndike, E. The fundamentals of learning. New York: Teachers College, Columbia University, 1932.

Tidyman, W., Smith, C., Butterfield, M. Teaching the language arts. New York: McGraw-Hill Book Company, 1969.

Toffler, A. Future shock. New York: Random House, 1970.

Toffler, A. Learning for tomorrow: The role of the future in education. New York: Random House, 1974.

Torrance, P.E. Guiding creative talent. Englewood Cliffs, N.J.: Prentice-Hall, 1962.

Trager, G., & Smith, H. Outline of English structure. Washington, D.C.: American Council of Learned Societies, 1965.

Trevarthen, C. Psychological action in early infancy. La Recherche (in press).

Tucker, G., & Lamber, W. The bilingual education of children. New York: Newbury House, 1972.

Valette, R. Developing and evaluating communication skills in the classroom. TESOL Quarterly, 1973, 7, 407-424.

Vygotsky, L.S. Thought and Language. Cambridge, Mass.: MIT Press, 1962.

Walden, J. Oral language and reading. Champaign, Ill.: National Council of Teachers of English, 1969.

Walen, H.L. Environments for English learning. Paper presented at the National Council for Teachers of English, 63rd Conference, Philadelphia, November 1973. (ERIC Document Reproduction Service No. ED 087 043)

Wasserman, M. Demystifying school: Writings and experiences. New York: Praeger Publishers, 1974.

Weber, L. The English infant school and informal education. Englewood Cliffs, N.J.: Prentice-Hall, Inc., 1971.

Weber, L. Cited in B. Blitz, The open classroom: Making it work. Boston: Allyn & Bacon, Inc., 1973.

Weinstein, G., & Fantani, M. Toward humanistic education: A curriculum of affect. New York: Praeger, 1970.

Weintraub, S. The Cloze procedure. Reading Teacher, 1968, 21, 567-571; 607.

Weir, R.H. Cited in M. Richards (Ed.), The integration of a child into a social world. New York: Cambridge University Press, 1974.

Weissman, C. Language assessment of EDC follow through children. EDC News, Winter 1976, pp. 10-11.

White, B. What makes children competent. Conference report at the Institute of Child Mental Health and the Planning Committee for Day Care Education, January 1974.

Whiting, B. Cuban refugees living in Naples blend two cultures. The Miami Herald, August 17, 1975.

Whiting, B., & Whiting, J. Children of six cultures: A psychoculture analysis. Boston: Harvard University Press, 1974.

White, R. Motivation reconsidered: The concept of competence. Psychological Review, 1959, 66, 297-333.

Whorf, B.L. A linguistic consideration of thinking in primitive communities. In J. Carroll (Ed.), Language, thought and reality. Cambridge, Mass.: Massachusetts Institute of Technology Press, 1956.

Williams, F. Language and poverty. Chicago: Markham, 1970.

Williams, J.P. Helping the bilingual child. In C. Braun (Ed.), Language, reading and the communication process. Newark, Del.: International Reading Association, 1971. (a)

Williams, J.P. The pre-adolescent boys and girls. In C. Braun (Ed.), Language, reading and the communication process. Newark, Del.: International Reading Association, 1971. (b)

Williams, R. Reading in the informal classroom. In E.B. Nyquist & G.R. Hawes, Open education: A sourcebook for parents and teachers. New York: Bantam Books, Inc., 1972.

Winnicott, D.W. The maturational processes and the facilitating environment. London: The Hogarth Press, 1965.

Winnicott, D.W. The family and individual development. London: Tavistock Publications, 1969.

Wittmer, J., & Myrick, R. Facilitative teaching: Theory and practice. Pacific Palisades, Calif.: Goodyear Publishing Company, Inc., 1974.

World Scope Encyclopedia. New York: Universal Guild, Inc., 1958.